Theology and Scriptural Imagination

Theology and Scriptural Imagination

Edited by L. Gregory Jones and James J. Buckley

Blackwell Publishers Ltd

Copyright © Blackwell Publishers Ltd

First published in 1998

Blackwell Publishers Ltd
108 Cowley Road, Oxford OX4 1JF, UK

and
350 Main Street
Malden, MA 02148, USA

British Library Cataloguing in Publication Data

A CIP catalogue record for this book is available from
the British Library

Library of Congress Cataloging-in-Publication Data

Data applied for

ISBN 978-0-631-21075-7

MIX
Paper from
responsible sources
FSC® C013604

CONTENTS

THEOLOGY AND SCRIPTURAL IMAGINATION

Editorial Introduction

Students of modern theology will not have to be reminded of the challenges to Scriptural imagination presented by traditional or contemporary abuses of Scripture: the use of Scripture to legitimate racism and sexism and more petty crimes; the haughty claims of some historical criticism and philosophical hermeneutics to understand Scripture better than it understands itself; and theological conspiracy with these imaginative powers of this world. The best response to such challenges comes as Christians gather around the Word to absorb its consolations and criticisms in their personal and corporate lives as the communion of saints. But students of Scripture in colleges and universities, seminaries and divinity schools must also be servants of the Word if Scriptural imagination is to thrive.

To this end, we have brought together biblical exegetes, historians of the interpretation of Scripture, as well as contemporary philosophers and theologians of various perspectives who, it seems to us, embody their own technical expertise as well as the sorts of imaginations it will take to celebrate the Word in season and out. Luke Johnson sets a tone as he suggests ways we can imagine the world Scripture imagines. David Dawson, against the background of the seductive pleas for anti-Jewishness during the German Church struggle, shows how figural reading of Scripture is tightly bound to the fashioning of Christian identity. Robert Wilken offers a different defense of allegory as a means for recovering traditional exegesis, and Kathryn Greene-McCreight shows how Scripture absorbs the world of John Calvin. Mary McClintock Fulkerson offers a feminist case for non-sexist interpretive communities, and Alvin Plantinga proposes how a Christian philosopher can challenge while taking advantage of Higher Biblical Criticism. Kathryn Tanner's essay is a fit conclusion, arguing that Scripture is more akin to a popular text than

L. Gregory Jones
James J. Buckley

high-culture classics, reminding us that Scriptural imagination is embodied as it is lived out by ordinary men and women.

As in previous volumes in this series, the essays here articulate overlapping as well as competing directions in modern theology. We hope that readers will seek out the common ground as well as the conflicts, to learn to taste the Word when it is bitter as well as sweet.

IMAGINING THE WORLD SCRIPTURE IMAGINES

LUKE TIMOTHY JOHNSON

If Scripture is ever again to be a living source for theology, those who practice theology must become less preoccupied with the world that produced Scripture and learn again how to live in the world Scripture produces. This will be a matter of imagination, and perhaps of leaping.

Imagining Worlds

All imagination is embodied. Images differ from concepts in the clay that clings to them. Scripture itself imagines a world. By imagining a world, Scripture brings it into being. Like all imaginative creations, the scriptural world is rooted in the physical realm where humans live. But the world conjured by Scripture is by no means simply to be identified with the physical realm where humans live and act.

For one thing, the world imagined by Scripture is considerably smaller than the human world. It is obvious that the spatial world of Scripture is tiny compared to the cosmos of Carl Sagan.[1] The temporal world of Scripture hardly is to be compared with the history of time, according to Stephen Hawking.[2] The world imagined by Scripture also is small when one considers the wide range of possible human activities. Scripture has a fairly limited sensibility. It is much concerned with law and morality, little with romance and affection, not at all with visual beauty.

In another way, the world of Scripture also is larger than that of ordinary human endeavor. Scripture imagines a world more richly furnished than our own, including angels and demons and assorted spirits of a sort not recognized by Sagan and Hawking. Most of all, its world contains (or perhaps is contained by) God, which makes it the biggest of all possible worlds.

Luke Timothy Johnson
Emory University, Atlanta, GA 30322, USA

Carl Sagan imagines, on the basis of evidence largely unavailable or unintelligible to most of us, a universe of immeasurable reach, yet he cannot imagine a God related to that great expanse.[3] Stephen Hawking imagines, on the basis of musings inaccessible to the rest of us, a universe of incomprehensible duration, yet he cannot imagine a God large enough to create that universe.[4] Despite its severe spatial and temporal limitations, the Scripture imagines (also on the basis of experiences and reports not within the common ken) a world in which every creature is at every moment summoned into being by a Power and Presence that is at once distant and close, ageless and instant.

No more than the scriptural world are the worlds imagined by Sagan and Hawking (and all those others who are summoned by these names) simply the "real world." Like the world imagined by Scripture, they are products of this particular physical space and time humans occupy and act within, but they are both less and more than this physical space and time. Their imaginings open up the human perception of the here and now. As a result, this moment and this place look different by being placed in a larger space and longer history. Likewise, our disposition of this item in this moment might also be different because of the perspective imagined for us. We now act thus and not so because we conceive the world to be constructed in this way and not that. The world constructed by Scripture also provides an opening to new perceptions of the here and now, and provides options for disposing of this and that in ways not otherwise imaginable. By imagining the world as always and essentially related to God, Scripture reveals the world and at the same time reveals God.

People act on the basis of the imagined world in which they dwell, and by acting on what they imagine, they help establish their worlds as real. Those acting on the imaginings of a Sagan or a Hawking make the world of Sagan and Hawking more real and less imaginary. So also those who act on the basis of the imaginary world of Scripture make it less imaginary and more real—a dream shared is a dream less in danger of disappearance. Living in any of these worlds requires a fundamental acceptance of its premises, an adjustment of vision according to its perceptions, and a decision to act as though these premises and perceptions were not only real but valid. Because Scripture imagines the world—the one in which we live and move —to have its source and sustaining in an Other who makes us live and move, we are able to inhabit the world from this perspective and decide to act on this premise. By so seeing and acting we turn the world imagined by Scripture into the real world in which we live and move.

Theology is what we call the effort of our minds to catch up with the work of the Living God in the world. Or, to put it in terms of the conceit here being pursued, theology is the name we give to the effort of our minds to grasp the world conjured by God and construed by Scripture.

Dear reader, by this point in the essay, you know very well what sort of intellectual game I am playing. Nothing could be more obvious than that the way I have laid this out reflects our loss of that world imagined by Scripture, for if we really inhabited it wholly, we could not speak of it as one world among others, as one more or less attractive option to be entertained; it would be, if we inhabited it wholly, simply our world. It is precisely our distance from this imaginative world that is our greatest deficit when it comes to doing theology.

The question I want to pose here is: to what degree does our contemporary study of Scripture increase rather than remove this impediment to theology, and what steps might theologians take to recover a properly scriptural imagination?

Living Cities And Lost Cities

Imagine the world constructed by Scripture as a living city that one might inhabit. This is not hard to imagine, after all, for in fact it was such a city for many and still remains so for some. How do people who have grown up and continue to live in such a city know it? Their knowledge is instinctive, connatural, geared to the practices of the city and its own peculiar ways. They understand how things are done in the city even if they cannot explain such customs to outsiders. They know how to get to places in the city quickly and easily even when they do not know the names of streets. They move about the city largely by means of images and landmarks which inform their every move even if they never consciously advert to them: a storefront here, a park bench there, a billboard hanging overhead.

Such knowledge is deep, intimate, non-systematic, comprehensive, practical. Natives of this city know in their bones the accents, nomenclature, handshakes and nods, the intricate timing of speech and silence, the type of things that outsiders can spend decades studying and memorizing and imitating, without ever getting them quite right. In a living city, the past is not someplace else, but this place; the city's past continues as part of its present. The past is not memorialized but incorporated. The city's history is not external to its inhabitants, but is part of their own story; indeed, their story cannot be told without telling the story of the city. They know the difference between the past and the present, but they make no artificial distinction between them: past and present are part of the same stream of life. Where there used to be trolley tracks now there are buses. Where there used to be stop signs now there are signal lights. Where there used to be a drug store now there is a boutique. Still, speech here continues the accents of the parents, and the feet of running children fall in the steps of their parents. In this city there is constant change, yet the change is contained within a deeper continuity, as this city remains, undeniably and indefinably, this and only this city.

Are there limits to this sort of knowledge? Yes. Are there dangers to the inhabitants' assumption that they are necessarily living in the same city simply because they occupy the same place? Of course. But these are the limits and dangers of life itself.

For much of the history of Christianity, the world imagined by Scripture was like such a living city. Patristic and Medieval authors—even writers through the Reformation and beyond—give no sense that they inhabit a world other than that imagined by Scripture.[5] It is their world. Nor is there any distinct gap between the study of Scripture and Theology. The two activities are virtually one, and have the same point: the glorification of God through the transformation of human behaviour according to the reality imagined by Scripture.[6]

Those theologians were not ignorant of the existence of other cities or their charms. They engaged Greek and Arabic Philosophers in debate.[7] Nor were they unaware of literary and theological difficulties in the text. These provided them with much of their entertainment.[8] But nowhere do we find the sense that these authors are visiting Scripture from some other place. Its turnings are their turnings. The rhythms of Scripture are, for the most part, their rhythms, Scripture's language is their language.[9] We do not find them pausing over the possible differences in the meaning of "grace" in Scripture and in their sermons, for it would not occur to them that there would be a difference. They saw the world as one in which grace was not a linguistic puzzle to be solved, but an experiential reality to be celebrated. In their city, they saw their steps fall on the prints made by James and Paul and John.

Cities can die and be covered over by sand. When cities disappear, the worlds of meaning within which so many lives were lived die also. Through archaeological exhumation, of course, some pieces and some sense of those cities can be recovered. In fact, the archaeologist can know the city in ways that none of its inhabitants ever did. The archaeologist can dig through the various strata of ruins, exposing to light and synchronic examination the changes in culture that none of its former inhabitants noticed. The archaeologist can date with some precision the stages of the city's former life, can mark the streets and houses with great precision, can uncover the systems of aqueducts and sewers, can compare this city at its various stages to other places similarly covered over and then uncovered. The archaeologist might even imagine what the people were like who created the city. But the one thing the archaeologist cannot do is actually imagine that city as its inhabitants imagined it when they walked its streets and argued in its halls and made love in its beds. The reason is that for the archaeologist, the past is always past and only past. It has nothing to do with the archaeologist's present and can make no claim on the archaeologist's future. The lost city is just one more city among others.

Since the triumph of the historical-critical method within biblical studies, the relationship of theology to Scripture has resembled that of an archaeologist to an ancient site. The historical-critical approach can, without any unfairness, be called a kind of literary archaeology.[10] It has been preoccupied with the precise detection of literary seams—equivalent to strata in an archaeological dig—and with the use of those seams as clues to the people who produced the literary evidences still visible, in order to trace a history of Israel and early Christianity. The enterprise is both difficult and hazardous. Like the archaeologist who is tempted to extrapolate a lost culture on the basis of too few shards, so Biblical diggers can grow overconfident in their capacity to detect layers, assign traditions, and imagine the circumstances that produced them.[11]

The intellectual curiosity driving the scientific dissection of past cultures is entirely legitimate. However, when that past culture is the world imagined by Scripture, something fundamental is revealed by this approach. No approach more clearly divides the world of Scripture from the examiner's world. The supreme virtue in exegesis as carried out within this scientific paradigm is to secure the "otherness" of the text, to avoid the crime of "eisegesis" by which contemporary perspectives are read anachronistically into an ancient and alien world. The methodologically postulated distance between these worlds was increasingly taken for granted as the study of the Bible became more and more a concern of the academy rather than a matter of personal and community transformation within the church. The community of readers who might have embodied the imaginative world of Scripture became themselves more and more disembodied, as the analysis of ancient texts took place in a context apart from the practices of piety.

Historical Hegemony

The historical-critical approach to the Bible drives a decisive wedge between the world imagined by Scripture and the world inhabited by its examiners. The entire paradigm is based on the premise that the two worlds are, in fact, different. When Christian theology bound itself over to the hegemony of the historical-critical method, it found itself only a visitor to the world it once called home. There is no intrinsic reason why historical reconstruction of the past should have any impact on theology. That it did was connected to the collapse of the world of Scripture—and of Scripture's God—into a world of Enlightenment sensibility which seemed larger at the time, even though in retrospect it, too, seems limited.[12] Christian practitioners of the historical-critical approach, however, have remained in a chronic state of denial concerning the true state of affairs, which is that the very notion of "approaching" the Bible as an artifact of a former age is the clearest confession imaginable that those so approaching come from "somewhere else," and that the scriptural world is no longer their own.

One expression of denial is found in those histories of early Christianity that were much less histories than theological salvage operations. Finding the earliest form of Christianity became important because of the mythic conviction that origins define essence. Within such a mythic understanding, later realization of the church was to be judged against the historically discovered origin. Above all, this myth provided a "criticism" for any form of Christianity that resembled Catholicism.[13] Securing that "historical essence" in Christian origins, however, came at considerable cost, namely, the jettisoning of huge amounts of the scriptural world in order to save a few pieces intact and usable.[14]

Rather than the theologian being first of all a student of Scripture, who could explore its world from within, confident that however much things had changed, its world also was the theologian's own, the theologian was now dependent on the historian's excavations of a world that was becoming increasingly foreign, not least because it was so regarded and so treated by the very method that purported to rescue its essential pieces. There were not, in fact, a great many pieces salvaged, and lacking the coherent imaginative world from which the pieces had been wrenched, it is not surprising that theology could do little with them.[15]

The quest for the historical Jesus stands as the classic expression of this odd misalliance between history and theology. Here the excavation of traditions explicitly set itself *against* the world imagined by Scripture and lived in by the Church in order to secure scientifically verifiable information about Jesus as a historical figure. The perspectives of the scriptural authors and of the majority of New Testament texts were eliminated by this quest, all in the name of proper historical method. And then, this historically reconstituted Jesus—not the Jesus imagined by the Gospels and celebrated by the Letters and contemplated by the Seer of Revelation, but a cardboard figure pasted together from scraps by a process utterly devoid of imagination—was supposed to function as a norm for Christian identity in the present![16]

The quest for the historical Jesus shows us the results of a sterile literalism that can neither engender a distinguishable Christian identity nor breathe life into its supposed subject. In its first, as in its current season, the quest presents the unedifying spectacle of Christian self-hatred: scholars unwilling to dwell in the world of Scripture but who are incapable of abandoning altogether that world. In its first, as in its present manifestation, the search for a usable Jesus is driven by the inability to imagine any longer the Jesus imagined by the Gospels.

Biblical Theology is a second way of trying to close the gap between historical criticism of the Bible and theology.[17] The very name indicates distance from the world of Scripture, for it suggests the possibility of a theology that is not biblical, and a study of the Bible that is not theological.[18] The many attempts at constructing a satisfactory biblical theology have succeeded mainly in revealing the contradictions inherent to the enterprise. Efforts to transcend history reveal how profoundly pervasive the historical perspective is.[19] The desire to unify diverse witnesses almost inevitably leads to eliminating some of Scripture's voices while privileging others, and to imposing a false harmony by means of some abstract category or principle.[20] Most of all, Biblical Theology manages to keep the world of Scripture firmly in the past, with its own mediational role alone emphasizing the distance between the world imagined by Scripture and the world inhabited by contemporary investigators.

Biblical Theology fails worst when it succeeds best. When theologians take up its distilled propositions or principles as "the biblical witness," the living conversation between theology and Scripture is not opened but closed. Biblical Theology remains primarily an academic exercise, a variety of the history of ideas or, perhaps, an ethnography of past cultures.[21] It neither derives life from the church nor specifically addresses the transformation of human lives within a community imagining itself to live within the world imagined by Scripture.

This, then, is our present situation, and it is not at all clear how we can make it better. Certainly there are no academic solutions available, at least not from within the guild of biblical studies. The study of Scripture within that profession has become simply a product of the academy and has explicitly distanced itself from the life of believers.[22] The very measure of its intellectual integrity is its degree of separation from confessional interests. The development of ideological criticism among biblical scholars only makes explicit the way in which they assume the moral superiority of the world they inhabit to the world imagined by Scripture. When the cross of Jesus Christ becomes a scandal, not because of the way it subverts worldly wisdom, but because it is perceived as a morally dangerous symbol, then theology's relationship with Scripture has become tenuous indeed.[23]

Recovering Imagination

Theology's recovery of a scriptural imagination must come from a relationship with Scripture that is mediated, not by a scholarly guild committed to historical reconstruction, but by a faith community whose practices are ordered to the transformation of humans according to the world imagined by Scripture—a world, faith asserts, which expresses the mind of God. This is the leap I spoke of in my opening paragraph. Perhaps it is better described as a turn mandated by the awareness that, whatever its intentions or virtues once might have been, the academic study of the Bible has, for the longest part of its career, been at best critical of the life of the church and at worst intensely hostile toward it.

I do not suggest that those located in academic settings cannot themselves undertake such a turn, but their doing so will require almost heroic effort, for they will be cutting against the grain of the academy's own increasingly distorted criteria and expectations. It is necessary, therefore, to encourage the development of theologians with scriptural imagination within the structures of the church itself.

Scripture as Imaginative World

I think there are at least four essential steps toward the recovery of scriptural imagination, once the turn has been made from the academic to the ecclesial setting. The first step is the most obvious and the most critical, namely, the appropriate apprehension of Scripture itself as a body of literature that does not primarily describe the world but rather imagines a world, and by imagining it, *reveals it*, and by revealing it, enables it to be brought into being within this physical space humans share with each other. Please note that I am not proposing a *sacrificium intellectus* by which we retreat to a biblical cosmology and psychology and pretend that they are adequate to our present day sense of science. Just the opposite: I suggest that we expand our minds by entering into the imaginative world of Scripture, for it is only within that world that we can learn of the God who creates us from nothing, interacts with us at every moment, knows us utterly, and saves us by granting us a share in God's own life through the death and resurrection of Jesus.[24]

Despite theories concerning expanding universes and evolving species, it still is possible, and indeed may be necessary, to imagine the world as a garden that God has planted for the delight of humans—a garden that humans, through ignorance and envy, have made into a place of deceit and death. It still is possible, and indeed may be necessary, to imagine the wood of the cross as the instrument of healing from that first mortal wound of disobedience in the garden.[25] But such imagining is available only to those who are willing to regard Scripture not as a source of propositions but as a vast collection of interwoven images.

To live within this imaginative world is not to flee reality but to constitute an alternative reality. This construal of the world does not contradict the worlds of science and philosophy because it does not compete with them. Scripture enables me to affirm that the universe is expanding and species are evolving and any number of other interesting if not compelling truths, and also to confess that precisely all this random and exciting movement derives from the God who says, "Let there be light." Scripture enables me to confess that in every point pertinent to human religious and moral behavior—that is to say, in every point really pertinent to being human—calling this universe (expanding or not) a garden planted by God works just fine.[26] Indeed, while the (presumed) truth of an expanding universe or evolving species translates only abstractly and arduously into a vision of the world bearing any moral valence, the moral implications of being given a garden to tend are obvious and immediate. Life and all of life's thoughts are not adequate to spell out what gardening the earth might mean.

The case of Jesus is instructive. The historical questers seek to fix the figure of Jesus in the past, and at the same time propose him as normative to the church.[27] Every such reconstruction, however, represents a narrowing, and therefore a distorting, of the multiple and rich images of Jesus throughout the pages of the New Testament. The life of faith in the community is generated and guided by the power of the Holy Spirit given by the resurrected Lord Jesus. The faith community, therefore, imagines itself in a world filled with the power of that resurrected life, and in the constant presence of the Living One through word, sacrament, fellowship, prayer and solidarity with the suffering. It celebrates this multiplicity of images even as it celebrates the diversity of its own experience of the risen Jesus.[28] It regards the effort to fix Jesus in history not only as impossible, but also as a little foolish and beside the point. The church lives within this set of convictions (or if you prefer this set of imaginings), however, only when it dwells within the world imagined by Scripture as a whole.

Communities of Practice
A second step toward a theology with scriptural imagination is the cultivation of communities of readers whose appropriation of Scripture is grounded in practices of Christian piety. Imagination, I have suggested, always is embodied. The imaginative world of Scripture must find embodiment in specific disciplines and practices. The most important of these, of course, is worship, not only because it expresses and enacts the world revealed by Scripture through praise of God, but also because it is through liturgical proclamation of the word in all of its forms that a scriptural ethos is formed among people.[29] But the practices of piety include also all of the transformative attitudes and behaviors associated with the Mind of Christ: sharing possessions; healing the sick; caring for the helpless; visiting those in prison; providing hospitality; praying alone and in common. Only in communities committed to the creation of such a transformed existence can the world imagined by Scripture find authentic hearing and expression.[30]

A community of readers committed to transformative practices of Christian piety allows for the imaginative reading of Scripture while holding in check the human potential for misguided fantasy and projection. In different ways, both the quest for the historical Jesus and Biblical Theology have sought to suppress the complexity, ambiguities and contradictions of Scripture by means of a univocal reading. If one is committed to a literal reading of Scripture, and if one allows for individual interpretation, then efforts to create a single authoritative reading are understandable and even necessary, for there is no other control except in the text itself. Thus, historical questers search for a Jesus who is clear and simple and without contradiction. Moreover, they construct a biblical theology that is clear and simple and without contradiction. Life itself, however, is not simple, nor clear, and has many contradictions. But within a reading community dedicated to the practice of Christian piety, neither the complexities of the text nor the ambiguities of experience need be feared. A community grounded in practices derived from Scripture and constantly nurtured by the wisdom communicated through the complex images and symbols of Scripture can be trusted to read with discrimination and discernment according to the Mind of Christ.[31]

This is especially so when the exercise of scriptural imagination by theologians within the community of faith is directed to the same transformation of mind and heart and practice. The difference for discourse about Christian morality, for example, can be startling. Scripture is read not simply as a source of rules for behavior—these are given already by the scripturally derived norms of the community—but as a source of wisdom and shaper of character.[32] Because the community is not dependent on the literal rendering of Scripture, it can embrace all of the richness of Scripture. In this case, as in others, structure is not the opposite of spontaneity but its prerequisite. There is, therefore, no more urgent task for theology than the creation of reading communities committed to the practices of Christian piety.

Learning to Read
The third step is re-engaging the rich world of image and metaphor within Scripture itself, allowing the imagination of the theologian, as the inhabitant of a familiar and well-loved city, to roam freely through the Sacred Writ. One of the most destructive results of the historical-critical method's hegemony over biblical studies has been its suppression of imagination in the name of literalism. In standard histories of interpretation, the fifteen hundred years of biblical interpretation within the church and based on the multiple levels of meaning in the text (the literal, the moral, the allegorical) are reduced to mere prologue, a "dark ages" of interpretation from which the Reformation and then the Enlightenment freed critics.[33] It was precisely the use of the imagination by such "pre-critical interpretation" that was regarded as dangerous. But if allegory had its excesses—and no reader of Gregory the Great would deny that it did—the complete suppression of any level of reading other than the literal was equally an overreaction.

No one way of reading is intrinsically superior to another. Rather, different ways of reading are better fitted to different purposes. If Scripture is being used to establish the moral norms of the community, then the literal sense (functionally that meaning most publicly available) is desirable, indeed demanded.[34] But if Scripture is being read in order to enliven the mind and the heart, or to expand the imagination, or simply to play contemplatively in the fields of the Lord, then multiple ways of reading are important, indeed imperative.

As *haggadah* was to *halakah* within classical Judaism, so allegory was to the literal meaning within classical Christianity.[35] For Rabbinic Judaism, *halakah* was a matter of determining community norms, how the people were to "walk" according to the commandments and place a hedge around Torah. It was a matter of great seriousness, demanding scholarship, attention to the minutiae of language, and ultimately some sort of authoritative decision (*din*) for a given time and place. However, because the central body of *mitzvoth* was so well and firmly established, so inarguable because of the weight of its antiquity and authority, such serious determinations were secondary to the reading and debating of Torah for purposes of wisdom and delight. This was the realm of *haggadah*, in which there was equal attention to the text, but also much greater freedom for the imagination. It is, naturally, in the realm of *haggadah* that we find the rich resources of Rabbinic theology and ethics (as in the *Pirque Aboth* and the *Aboth de Rabbi Nathan*). Within pre-Reformation—and even some post-Reformation—Christianity, allegorical interpretation (in the broadest sense of the term) played the same role, enabling the Scripture to become an entire world of type and figure, allusion and echo, wisdom and delight. Can anyone who has read Origen or Bernard of Clairvaux *On the Canticle of Canticles* not recognize the impoverishment to the Christian imagination that the loss of these homilies would represent?[36]

In response to the aridity of the historical-critical method, the Biblical Theology Movement recently recognized some of the intricate intertextual connections within the Bible, and sought to demonstrate them through the development of "biblical themes" and "biblical terms."[37] The effort unfortunately was subverted by faulty linguistic and cultural assumptions, and became an easy target for scornful attack.[38] These students of Scripture were correct in their conviction that the images of the Bible revealed a distinctive world, but were erroneous in connecting that distinctiveness to the character of "Hebrew Thought" as opposed to "Greek Thought."[39] Equally flawed was the assumption that meaning was carried by words rather than through phrases, sentences, and arguments. The adherents of the Biblical Theology Movement erroneously assumed that a comparison of all the uses of a particular word in the Bible would yield its full "theological meaning" that then might be read back into each instance of its use.[40]

Despite the legitimate criticism directed to such premises and procedures, the Biblical Theology Movement represented an attempt to get at a dimension of the biblical text that historical criticism consistently misses, precisely because it is preoccupied with the world which produced the text rather than the world the text produces. The world which the text produces is not simply a haphazard collection of compositions written by various authors speaking from and for diverse communities over a period of centuries, but it is also a complex network of literary interconnections established by the use and reuse of terms that gain depth and richness by means of intricate and subtle allusion. Attention to these interconnections is justified, therefore, because together they create a world of metaphoric structures within which humans can live in a distinctive manner.[41]

Think, for example, of the pervasive scriptural metaphor of "the way." It has its basis in the physical world of nomadism. For the nomad moving in the right direction to find water, shelter or food literally was to walk in the way of life, just as moving away from water or shelter or food literally was to walk in a way leading to death. The combination of movement, direction, goal, and consequence enabled the term "way" to function metaphorically for human behavior itself.[42] As such, we find this metaphor everywhere in

Scripture and in the moral·literature of Christianity. It can be used to express the simple contrast between patterns of behavior ("the way of light/life" versus "the way of darkness/death"). It also suggests the possibility of "wandering" from a way, and "turning back" to a way. Perhaps most elaborately, the metaphor of the way fits within the complex imagery of pilgrimage, so that the (already complex) physical movement from a profane place to a sacred place, or from diaspora to homeland, becomes an image of human life as a whole, moving from mortal life in an alien environment to a heavenly homeland.

The metaphor of "the way" is a basic metaphor that organizes a complex system of subsidiary images and metaphors that depend on its maintaining its radical character for their own life and effectiveness.[43] The metaphor also contains an implicit but comprehensive view of reality.[44] Imagining human existence as "being on the way" toward God has the most profound corollaries for every sort of human endeavor: earthly existence is relative, temporary, and preparatory, in comparison with a life with God that is ultimate, eternal, and perfect. Such an understanding encourages a diaspora ethics of itinerary, detachment, dispossession, solidarity and endurance in suffering, rather than a homeland ethics of stability, engagement, acquisition, and human fulfillment in the present life. It engenders a passover spirituality of "crossing over" from death to life through the bearing of other's burdens on the way; it does not easily support a spirituality of finding or centering the self.

The term "way" does not bear all these connotations by itself; the same metaphor, in fact, might have quite different connotations in another imaginary world, as the expression "the Beauty Way" does within Navaho spirituality. Note also that the term does not have its full meaning in any single instance of its use, as though the metaphor always was operative for each of the biblical authors. Just the opposite: the term emerges as metaphorical and therefore as world-orienting only for the person who reads the Scripture in its entirety, and as directed to the transformation of human identity only within communities committed to the practices of Christian piety. Indeed, the analysis of individual sentences, passages, or books, will not uncover the force of the metaphor. It exists and exercises its power over the Christian imagination precisely as part of the world imagined by Scripture as a whole.

The metaphor of "the way" is, as we know, only one of many such basic metaphors in Scripture. I have provided another earlier in this essay, namely, that of the garden. It is apparent at once that these metaphors stand in tension with each other. Living within the imagined world of Scripture does not mean living without tension or contradiction; it means resolving contradictions and tensions in creative, and equally metaphorical ways. For instance, the image of the earth as garden has been incorporated into the metaphor of the way, so that "Paradise Lost" expresses the human sense of exile, while the image of "Paradise Restored" stands at the end of the journey.

Such metaphors are the more powerful when they are embodied in specific practices of the church. The image of a people on pilgrimage is obviously more persuasive when congregations move in liturgical procession through streets and fields on rogation days, chanting the litany of all those saints who form "the cloud of witnesses" waiting at the end of their journey toward God, or when they follow the "light of Christ" that is the Paschal Candle through the darkened nave at the Easter Vigil, or when they visit the sick and elderly to bring the eucharistic bread as *viaticum,* or when they pray in the manner of the *Cloud of Unknowing* or the *Way of the Pilgrim,* or when they walk through the streets seeking the homeless and providing them with shelter in their church building. Such practices of piety make the metaphor of "being on the way" an interpretation of lived human experience, and brings the world imagined by Scripture into existence by embodying it in the physical space we humans share with each other.

Connecting with Experience
A fourth step toward recovering a scriptural imagination within theology— and a necessary one if attention to literary interconnections is not to become simply another intellectual or aesthetic game—is paying attention to actual human experience in the world. If theology is the effort of our minds to catch up with the work of the Living God in the world, then attention must be paid to the human stories within which that work is enacted. Part of con- temporary theology's impoverished sense of God's presence is due to its inattention to the places where that presence is most obvious, namely, in the human drama of idolatry and sin, grace and faith. As that drama is played out in every human story, it becomes, if properly heard, revelatory.[45] The same inattention to the human experience of God characterizes the reading of Scripture within the biblical guild.[46] Yet the experience of the Living God is the most obvious element in the construction of the imaginary world of Scripture. Moreover, the claim to have experienced the *same* Living God through the Lord Jesus Christ was the most compelling reason for joining two disparate collections of compositions into a single anthology called Scripture. And it is the possibility of experiencing that same Living God in the world today that makes the doing of Christian theology anything more than a sterile academic exercise.

Here, then, is the most fundamental turning away from the imaginary worlds of the Sagans and the Hawkings toward the imaginary world of Scripture, the most fundamental step toward a theology with scriptural imagination: to live in this world as one created at every moment by an unseen Power who drenches us with grace and transforms us into God's own image, and to regard our own story and every story we hear within that world as truth.[47] Imagine that.

NOTES

1 See Carl Sagan, *Pale Blue Dot: A Vision of the Human Future in Space* (New York, NY: Random House, 1994).
2 See Stephen Hawking, *A Brief History of Time: From the Big Bang to Black Holes* (New York, NY: Bantam Books, 1988).
3 Sagan, pp. 11–57.
4 Or at least, a God who is not constrained by the universe itself; see Hawking, pp. 7–9, 116, 141, 174.
5 See George A. Lindbeck, *The Nature of Doctrine: Religion and Theology in a Post-Liberal Age* (Philadelphia, PA: Westminster Press, 1988), pp. 112–124.
6 This recently has been demonstrated with great effectiveness by William Placher, *The Domestication of Transcendence: How Modern Theology Went Wrong* (Louisville, KY: Westminster Press, 1996), pp. 22–68.
7 See Augustine, *Civitas Dei* VIII; Thomas Aquinas, *Summa Contra Gentiles* I, 60–63; I, 71.
8 Patristic readers of the Letter of James, for example, not only recognized the tension between James 2:14–26 and Gal. 3:16 that so exercised Luther (see Zachary the Rhetorician, *Capita Selecta ex Historicae Ecclesiasticae* IX [PG 85:1176–1178]), but also that between James 1:13 and Deut. 13:3 (see Eucherius of Lyons, *Instructionum Liber* I, 2 [PL 50:810]).
9 See Lindbeck, p. 118: "It is the text, so to speak, which absorbs the world, rather than the world the text."
10 The analogy is scarcely original; see, e.g., James A. Sanders, *From Sacred Story to Sacred Text: Canon as Paradigm* (Philadelphia, PA: Fortress Press, 1987), p. 79.
11 See Luke T. Johnson, "On Finding the Lukan Community: A Cautious Cautionary Essay," *1979 SBL Seminar Papers* ed. P. Achtemeier (Missoula, MT: Scholars Press, 1979), pp. 87–100, and "The Search for the (Wrong) Jesus," *Bible Review* 11/6 (November, 1995), pp. 20–25, 44.
12 See Placher, pp. 71–107.
13 See Jonathan Z. Smith's devastating analysis of how theological presuppositions in the study of Christian origins were dominated by the fear of "pagano-papism," in *Drudgery Divine: On the Comparison of Early Christianities and the Religions of Antiquity* (Chicago Studies in Judaism; Chicago, IL: University of Chicago Press, 1990), pp. 1–35, 114–115.
14 The principle of "content criticism" and its corollary of a "canon within the canon" suggested by Luther's comments on James in his "Preface to the New Testament" of 1522 (*Luther's Works 35: Word and Sacrament*, ed. E. T. Bachmann [Philadelphia, PA: Fortress Press, 1960] p. 362), has led to results Luther never could have imagined in writings such as Robert Funk, *Honest to Jesus: Jesus for a New Millennium* (San Francisco, CA: HarperSanFrancisco, 1996), pp. 103–120.
15 It is painful to observe how little positive content can be drawn from the New Testament by one committed to the presuppositions I have sketched; see, e.g., Willi Marxsen, *New Testament Foundations for Christian Ethics*, trans. O. C. Dean, Jr. (Minneapolis, MN: Fortress Press, 1993).
16 See Luke T. Johnson, *The Real Jesus: The Misguided Quest for the Historical Jesus and the Truth of the Traditional Gospels* (San Francisco, CA: HarperSanFrancisco, 1996).
17 For a good orientation, see Steven J. Kraftchick, Charles D. Myers, and Ben C. Ollenburger, *Biblical Theology: Problems and Prospects* (Nashville, TN: Abingdon Press, 1995).
18 See Hendrik Boers, *What is New Testament Theology?: The Rise of Criticism and the Problem of a Theology of the New Testament* (Philadelphia, PA: Fortress Press, 1979).
19 See Brevard S. Childs, *Biblical Theology of the Old and New Testaments: Theological Reflections on the Christian Bible* (Minneapolis, MN: Fortress Press, 1992), and my review, "The Crisis in Biblical Scholarship," *Commonweal* 120/21 (December 3, 1993), pp. 18–21. Even more startling is the decision to make the "historical Jesus" a key element for New Testament theology in George Caird, *New Testament Theology*, completed and edited by L. D. Hurst (Oxford: Clarendon Press, 1994), pp. 345–408, and in Richard B. Hays, *The Moral Vision of the New Testament: A Contemporary Introduction to New Testament Ethics* (San Francisco, CA: HarperSanFrancisco, 1996), pp. 158–168.
20 See Nils A. Dahl, "Rudolf Bultmann's Theology of the New Testament," in *The Crucified Messiah and Other Essays* (Minneapolis, MN: Augsburg Press, 1974), pp. 90–128, and my

review of Hays' *Moral Vision*, "Why Scripture is Not Enough," *Commonweal* 124/11 (June 6, 1997), pp. 23–25.

21 This is the approach taken by Wayne A. Meeks, *The Origins of Christian Morality: The First Two Centuries* (New Haven, CT: Yale University Press, 1993), pp. 9–17.

22 See Jon D. Levenson, *The Hebrew Bible, the Old Testament, and Historical Criticism* (Louisville, KY: Westminster/John Knox Press, 1993).

23 Delores Williams, *Sisters in the Wilderness: The Challenge of Womanist God-Talk* (New York, NY: Orbis Books, 1993), pp. 143–177; for a more positive feminist view of the cross, see Sally B. Purvis, *The Power of the Cross: Foundations for a Christian Feminist Ethic of Community* (Nashville, TN: Abingdon Press, 1993).

24 See Luke T. Johnson, *Faith's Freedom: A Classic Spirituality for Contemporary Christians* (Minneapolis, MN: Fortress Press, 1990), pp. 15–59, where I suggest that the peculiar challenge to faith today is to oscillate between worlds constructed by secular analyses and the world constructed by Scripture.

25 I am playing with Genesis and Paul and John Wisdom, "The Logic of God," in *Paradox and Discovery* (Oxford: Basil Blackwell, 1965), pp. 1–22.

26 A wonderful example of this sort of approach is Sara Maitland's *A Big-Enough God: A Feminist's Search for a Joyful Theology* (New York, NY: Henry Hold and Company, 1995), esp. pp. 25–67.

27 Johnson, *The Real Jesus*, pp. 1–56.

28 This is the basic argument of Luke T. Johnson, *Learning Jesus: A Gospel-Centered Spirituality* (in press).

29 See Don E. Saliers, *Worship as Theology: Foretaste of Glory Divine* (Nashville, TN: Abingdon Press, 1994), pp. 21–38.

30 My point here is similar to that argued by Stanley Hauerwas in *Unleashing the Scripture: Freeing the Bible from Captivity to America* (Nashville, TN: Abingdon Press, 1993).

31 See Luke T. Johnson, *Scripture and Discernment: Decision-Making in the Church* (Nashville, TN: Abingdon Press, 1996), esp. pp. 109–132.

32 See my review of Hays' *Moral Vision* in *Commonweal*.

33 The classic example is W. G. Kümmel, *The New Testament: The History of the Investigation of Its Problems*, trans. S. Maclean Gilmore and Howard C. Kee (Nashville, TN: Abingdon Press, 1972), which devotes only seven pages (pp. 13–19) to the patristic and medieval periods!

34 See the discussion in Hans W. Frei, "The 'Literal Reading' of Biblical Narrative in the Christian Tradition: Does it Stretch or Will it Break?" in *Theology and Narrative: Selected Essays*, eds. George Hunzinger and William C. Placher (New York, NY: Oxford University Press, 1993), pp. 117–152.

35 These remarks extend the analogy developed in Luke T. Johnson, *The Writings of the New Testament: An Interpretation* (Philadelphia, PA: Fortress Press, 1986), pp. 547–548, and *Scripture and Discernment*, pp. 34–44. Compare Hauerwas, "Stanley Fish, the Pope, and the Bible," in *Unleashing the Scripture*, pp. 19–38.

36 It is important to note as well that Origen located his allegorical readings firmly within the creed-based general practice of the community; see *On First Principles* I, Preface, and IV, 1–2.

37 Some classic examples: Jaques Guillet, *Themes of the Bible*, trans. Albert J. LaMothe, Jr. (Notre Dame, IN: Fides Publishers, 1961); Albert Gelin, *The Poor Yahweh*, trans. Kathryn Sullivan (Collegeville, MN: Liturgical Press, 1964); Delbert R. Hillers, *Covenant: The History of a Biblical Idea* (Baltimore, MD: Johns Hopkins University Press, 1969).

38 Seldom has a book had the impact of James Barr's *Semantics of Biblical Language* (Philadelphia, PA: Trinity Press International, 1991).

39 Indeed, this is the perfect example of "theology" being dependent on a flawed reading of historical evidence; one of the greatest contributions of historical biblical scholarship over the past several decades has been to tear down the walls that were assumed to exist between Judaism and Hellenism.

40 Although such was not the purpose of *The Theological Dictionary of the New Testament*, ed. Gerhard Kittel, trans. Geoffrey Bromiley (10 volumes; Grand Rapids, MI: Wm. B. Eerdmans Publishing Company, 1964–1976), this has been the effect on many who have used it.

41 The ideas here are similar to those found in George Lakoff and Mark Johnson, *Metaphors We Live By* (Chicago, IL: University of Chicago Press, 1980), pp. 14–68.

42 See Lakoff and Johnson, pp. 41–45.
43 Ibid., pp. 87–105.
44 See Mark Turner, *The Literary Mind* (New York, NY: Oxford University Press, 1996), pp. 85–115.
45 Johnson, *Scripture and Discernment*, pp. 135–165.
46 See Luke T. Johnson, *Religious Experience: The Missing Dimension in New Testament Studies* (Minneapolis, MN: Fortress Press, 1998).
47 Two recent works in theology that possess the sort of scriptural imagination imagined here (and therefore provide hope) are: Miroslav Volf, *Exclusion and Embrace: The Gospel and the Other* (Nashville, TN: Abingdon Press, 1996), and William M. Thompson, *The Struggle for Theology's Soul: Contesting Scripture in Christology* (New York, NY: Crossroad Publishing, 1996).

FIGURAL READING AND THE FASHIONING OF CHRISTIAN IDENTITY IN BOYARIN, AUERBACH AND FREI

JOHN DAVID DAWSON

In December of 1933, less than one month before Hitler formally assumed the Chancellorship of Germany, Cardinal Michael Faulhaber, Archbishop of Munich, delivered a series of Advent sermons in St. Michael's Cathedral. Faulhaber opened his first sermon, "The Religious Values of the Old Testament and their Fulfillment in Christianity," by observing that "already in the year 1899, on the occasion of an anti-Semitic demonstration at Hamburg," "a demand was raised for the total separation of Judaism from Christianity, and for the complete elimination from Christianity of all Jewish elements."[1] Even more alarming to Faulhaber, though, was that now, in 1933, the "single voices" of 1899 had "swelled together into a chorus: Away with the Old Testament!"[2] To criticize Jews and Judaism was one thing, but to criticize the Old Testament was something else altogether. And to allow criticism of the Old Testament to escalate into an attack on German Christianity was intolerable. It simply is not true, insists Faulhaber, that "a Christianity which still clings to the Old Testament is a Jewish religion, irreconcilable with the spirit of the German people."[3] "When antagonism to the Jews of the present day is extended to the sacred books of the Old Testament, and Christianity is condemned because it has relations of origin with pre-Christian Judaism," then, declares Faulhaber, "the bishop cannot remain silent."[4]

The bishop, who was also Professor of Old Testament Scripture at the University of Strasbourg, asks his congregation to distinguish between Israel

John David Dawson
Religion Department, Haverford College, Haverford, PA 19041, USA

before and Israel after the death of Christ. The only Israel that matters for Christians is the one that existed up to the death of Christ:

> Before the death of Christ during the period between the calling of Abraham and the fullness of time, the people of Israel were the vehicle of Divine Revelation ... After the death of Christ Israel was dismissed from the service of Revelation. She had not known the time of her visitation. She had repudiated and rejected the Lord's Anointed, had driven Him out of the city and nailed Him to the Cross. Then the veil of the Temple was rent, and with it the covenant between the Lord and His people.[5]

The rent veil of the Temple, understood as a symbol of the annulment of God's covenant with Israel, renders the term "Israel" inapplicable to Christians. Ironically, it is only pre-Christian Judaism that has any Christian significance for Faulhaber. As for post-Christian Judaism—implicitly presented as a religion of the Talmud, not the Old Testament—nothing more need be said. And there is certainly no continuous Israel in which both Jews and Christians might continue to have a stake.

Faulhaber's concern is neither Judaism nor Israel but the validity of the Old Testament as part of the Christian Bible. To preserve the Christian significance of this text, he simply detaches it from Judaism; although "pre-Christian Judaism", "among all the nations of antiquity", has "exhibited the noblest religious values", it "did not produce those values of itself"—"The Spirit of the Lord enlightened them."[6] The books of the Old Testament, Faulhaber declares, "were not composed by Jews; they are inspired by the Holy Ghost."[7] Faulhaber does not attend to one ominous interpretative and ethical implication of his contrast in authorship: that reading Hebrew Scripture "according to the Spirit" that inspired its composition might suppress the concrete representation of the persons depicted in the text, and that such hermeneutical suppression might foreshadow the physical oppression of contemporary Jews. It is sometimes argued that orthodox Christian allegorical interpretation of Hebrew Scripture, as a response to Marcion's second century elimination of Hebrew Scripture from the Christian Bible, indicates that Christianity is fundamentally opposed to the sort of anti-Semitic impulses that Faulhaber presents his sermons as resisting. But Faulhaber's dispute with anti-Semitic "German Christians" is not a dispute about anti-Semitism but about Christian attitudes toward the Old Testament. His dispute highlights the radical difference between ensuring the continued existence of Jews and ensuring the continued Christian validity of the Old Testament: to save the text, some are prepared to sacrifice the people. Hence, Faulhaber does not plead for Christians to stop antagonizing their Jewish neighbors. Instead, he argues that "antagonism to the Jews of to-day must not be extended to the books of pre-Christian Judaism."[8] The Old Testament, he suggests, can retain a purely Christian significance only when Judaism has been eliminated from it. Once Judaism has been completely displaced from the Christian Bible, would Jews have any place in a Christian nation? Faulhaber believes he has removed a key impediment to a Christian nation of loyal Germans without Jews: "from the Church's point of view," he writes, "there is no objection whatever to racial research and race culture. Nor is there any objection to the endeavor to keep the national characteristics of a people as far as possible pure and unadulterated, and to foster their national spirit by emphasis upon the common ties of blood which unite them."[9] But when spirit becomes blood, commonality becomes sameness—and sameness has no tolerance, let alone respect, for difference.

I

At the time of his Advent sermons, Faulhaber was regarded by many as a voice of moderation. Today, Christians can only shudder at his conception of what the gospel implies about Jews and about Judaism's relation to Christianity. Just what is the unholy logic behind Faulhaber's reading of the Old Testament? A key assumption lies in his claim that the books of the Old Testament "were not composed by Jews" but were "inspired by the Holy Ghost" (or Spirit). Freed from identification with Judaism, that Spirit overcomes the particularities of the Old Testament text in order to make it palatable to "the spirit of the German people". Yet in disassociating Judaism from Christianity, Cardinal Faulhaber reverses the logic of the apostle Paul. In his Letter to the Romans, Paul traces the genealogy of what he regards as the true or spiritual Israel, which begins with Abraham and continues down to those Jews of Paul's own day who, like Paul himself, have become Christians. This true Israel, represented by the patriarchs and prophets who proclaimed Christ's coming through types and figures, is the trunk of the olive tree from which the branches of so-called "hardened" Israel have been broken off and into which gentile believers in Christ have been recently grafted. God's final purpose will have been fulfilled when, in some indefinite future, hardened Israel will come to accept Jesus as the Messiah, and the broken branches will be grafted back into the trunk of the true Israel (Rom. 11:17-24). Although Faulhaber acknowledges Paul's confidence in the future conversion of the Jews—"one day, at the end of time, for them too the hour of grace will strike (Rom. xi,26)"[10]—Israel no longer has any meaning for the interim: Faulhaber has dropped altogether Paul's metaphor of the engrafting of gentile Christians into the single trunk of true Israel now continued by Jewish Christians.

Different Christian interpretations of Israel have sponsored radically different consequences: one interpretation transformed a sect of Judaism into a new, world religion; another sought to transform that world religion into a world without Jews. If there is a line between Paul and Faulhaber, it is very thin, traced out only by Paul's insistence on understanding the term Israel as

the one community of Jews and gentiles who believe that Jesus of Nazareth
is the Messiah promised by God. Not everyone thinks a line exists between
these two understandings of Israel. In *A Radical Jew: Paul and the Politics of
Identity*, Daniel Boyarin argues that Paul, in pursuing the first interpretation
of "Israel", has already taken the crucial step toward the second.[11] Boyarin
observes that traditional religious Jews find Paul's claim to have discerned a
"spiritual" Israel consisting of those who practice a circumcision of the heart
as "inward Jews" to be contradictory, if not offensive: a Judaism devoid of
its most central self-identifying physical practices is simply not Judaism—
no matter how often it might call itself the "new" or "true" Israel. Boyarin
traces Paul's point of view back to the way he interprets Scripture. Paul, he
argues, is an allegorical interpreter, by which he means that Paul takes Jewish texts (along with the practices they describe) and gives them non-literal
meanings: hence physical circumcision becomes a non-physical, spiritual circumcision. Boyarin argues that this allegorical procedure has the pernicious
consequence of erasing the specific, concrete differences that identify what is
being read allegorically. Paul can declare in his Letter to the Galatians that
"in Christ there is neither Jew nor Gentile" only because he has, through his
allegorical reading of Hebrew Scripture, obliterated the literal descriptions
of the distinctive physical practices that serve to fashion the unique identity
of Jews.

Central to Boyarin's analysis is Paul's contrast between *gramma* and
pneuma ("letter" and "spirit" as traditionally translated). In letters to various
churches, Paul repeatedly contrasts *gramma* unfavorably with *pneuma*.
Perhaps his most influential formulation of the opposition between them
appears in his Second Letter to the Corinthians, where he declares that "God
has made us competent as ministers of a new covenant, a covenant not of the
gramma but of the *pneuma*; for the *gramma* kills, but the *pneuma* gives life"
(2 Cor. 3:6). Over the centuries, translators have rendered *gramma* differently. As for 2 Corinthians 3:6, Jerome translated *gramma* by *littera*; King
James's 17th century translators followed Jerome's lead, rendering *gramma*
as "letter"—"the letter killeth, but the spirit giveth life." The decision of
Jerome and the King James translators proved fateful, for *littera* is the basis
not only of "letter" but also of "literal". Translating *gramma* ("what is written")
as "letter" helps one easily (however wrongly) to the conclusion that when
Paul speaks of *gramma* in opposition to *pneuma*, he is contrasting a literal
with a non-literal interpretation of the same text.

Boyarin understands the contrast between *gramma* and *pneuma* to be a
wholly antithetical "binary opposition". In a binary opposition, to have A
means you must eliminate B, and vice-versa: to have "the spirit" (the allegorical or non-literal meaning of the text), one must give up the "letter" (the
text's literal meaning). The literal meaning is superseded by the allegorical,
and once Christians claim for themselves (and deny to Jews who will not
convert to Christianity) the capacity to read Jewish Scriptures allegorically,

Jewish Scripture and Judaism find themselves superseded by the Christian Old Testament and Christianity. Although Boyarin's book is about Paul, he makes it clear through his assimilation of Pauline, Origenist, and Augustinian hermeneutics that he regards the Pauline allegorical impulse as central to traditional Christianity's supersessionist relation to Judaism. Boyarin's analysis of Paul can be extended easily to Faulhaber, whose divorce of the text (the Old Testament) from the people (the Jews) is made possible by the separation of the "spirit" of the text from its "letter". Faulhaber's way of reading the Bible unfolds in allegiance to his own understanding of Paul's contrast of a literal *gramma* and a non-literal *pneuma* as binary oppositions: "the *gramma* kills, but the *pneuma* gives life."

But the translation of *gramma* as letter, which is the basis for understanding it as non-literal meaning, is simply inaccurate. In Paul's epistles, *gramma* simply means, to use his own phrase, "that which has been *eggegrammenê*," i.e., written or inscribed. Yet even though Paul's contrast between *gramma* and *pneuma* is surely not a contrast between literal and non-literal meaning, it is a contrast between two ways of reading Scripture (which for Paul meant Hebrew Scripture in the Septuagint translation). Paul argues that when one reads Hebrew Scripture "according to the *pneuma*", one reads it as the Old Testament—as Christian Scripture—which means that one reads it as prophesying or prefiguring Jesus as the Messiah. On the other hand, if one reads Hebrew Scripture "according to the *gramma*", one fails to discern its prefigurative, Christian import. For Paul, these two ways of reading Scripture entail a particular conception of the relationship between Judaism and Christianity. Those who live according to the *pneuma* cease to practice the prescriptions of the Torah, as Paul writes in his Letter to the Romans: "But now we are discharged from the law, dead to that which held us captive, so that we serve not under the old *gramma* but in the new life of the *pneuma*" (Rom. 7:6). And yet those who live according to the *pneuma* are said to continue to keep the law, but in a different way, as Paul writes in the same letter: "He is a Jew who is one inwardly, and circumcision is a matter of the heart, in the *pneuma* and not in the *gramma*" (Rom. 2:29). Here we have arrived at one of the most perplexing of Paul's beliefs: Christianity, a matter of life and reading "in the *pneuma*", is described as the life of Judaism, but the life of an "inward" Judaism in which the specific ritual practices that define Judaism are no longer performed in their usual bodily fashion but have become, in Tocqueville's not unrelated phrase, "habits of the heart". Amazingly, Paul's "inward" Jews, otherwise known as Christians, regarded themselves as the continuation of "true" Israel.

There is no question that Boyarin has sketched out with single-minded intensity one side of Paul's thinking, in which the apostle expresses the discontinuity between the religion in which he was raised and the one into which he was converted. But Boyarin under-represents the other side of Paul's thought, namely, Christianity's continuity with Judaism.[12] In order to consider the other, countervailing side of Christian reading of the Old Testament, I turn next to a Jewish scholar of an earlier generation—the German Romance philologist Erich Auerbach, probably the most influential non-Christian interpreter of Christian spiritual (or as he preferred to call it, figural) interpretation of the Old Testament.

II

Forced out of Germany in 1935 into exile in Istanbul, Auerbach published his seminal essay "Figura" in 1938 and began work on his magisterial book *Mimesis* in 1942.[13] With so much of his own western European world suddenly stripped from him, Auerbach sought to reweave that world textually, out of close readings of some classic texts of the western literary canon. In *Mimesis*, he would chart the history of western European forms of representing reality from Homer and the Bible to Virginia Woolf in order to paint a picture of a unified European culture of humanism that was already dissolving before his eyes. His work would be more than a memorialization or monumentalization of the past, however; it would also be an exercise in social and cultural criticism. Auerbach would write in order to tell his fellow Europeans that in joining Faulhaber and his opponents, they were directly contradicting their identity as Christians, *and therefore* as Europeans. Auerbach's argument was subtle and unique: secular European cultural unity was rooted in a uniquely religious mode of representing reality—the Christian tradition of figural interpretation of the Bible. Europe no longer recognized the true character of that tradition, or acknowledged its indebtedness to it. Horrendous betrayal—of the text and of one another—was the consequence.

To make his case about the true character of Christian figural interpretation, Auerbach needed access to the ancient writings of the Church Fathers. But the scholarly resources of the Turkish State University, where he was employed, were meager at best. In his "Epilogue to *Mimesis* ", he relates that he was given permission to use the set of Migne's *Patrologia* in the nearby Dominican Monastery, San Pietro di Galata. Special permission to use this collection had been granted to him by the Vatican apostolic delegate, Monsignor Angelo Roncalli. Like Faulhaber, Roncalli would soon become a Cardinal; later on, he would be better known as Pope John XXIII.[14] What Auerbach believed he had discovered in the pages of the San Pietro di Galata *Patrologia* was something not in evidence in Faulhaber's sermons: a rich tradition of Christian figural reading of the Old Testament in which the historical reality of ancient Jews had been preserved rather than superseded.

What kind of reading preserves the historical reality of what a text depicts? Auerbach first implores readers not to allow the meanings of words to replace the distinctive graphic character of the words themselves. Consider the following analogy. I look at one of the leaves hanging from a branch on the tree just outside my window. For some reason, I look at it with more than my usual level of attention. I am struck by its various details: streak of red right there, on the bottom of one of the three points; a mottling on the yellow portion above; several small holes near the stem. Soon I am absorbed in contemplation of the utterly unique features of that single leaf. There is not another one like it, I am sure. Then someone calls from across the room: "What are you looking at?" "A leaf," I answer. And now all uniqueness vanishes: I have been looking at "a leaf", an instance of that general class called "leaves". Does "a leaf" have three points or four? Is it red or green? In fact, does "a leaf" even exist in the world at all? Well, no, not really: just as there are no trees in general, there are no leaves as such. I had encountered a unique individual, but when asked to convey what I encountered, I handed over a general concept.[15] But my interlocutor is satisfied: he has, she concludes, been looking at a leaf. The wind suddenly snaps the stem, the leaf flutters away. Unimpeded by its absence, she and I go on talking about leaves, trees, autumn, the seasons. Reading the Old Testament, suggests Auerbach, can so easily be like that. We come across specific words on the page, and together those words paint a picture or define a character. What, we may ask, is the meaning of that picture? What is the author trying to say to us by describing that character in this way? What is the meaning, what is the point? And quietly, inadvertently, with the best of intentions, we begin to translate the text we are reading into something else until, finally, we are no longer reading the text at all. A form of reading that would preserve the historical reality of those things that a text depicts would need to begin, then, by preserving the graphic character of the words that render them for us.

But how does preserving the graphic character of biblical words help preserve the reality of those actual persons or events they depict? To begin with, Auerbach draws little distinction between the Bible as a literary text and the Bible as a historical document: he refers to the Bible as *littera-historia* or letter-history—a single text that describes actual past persons and events as significant. As some philosophers of history have recently argued, past persons and events are not significant in themselves; rather, it is the historian's deliberate, narrative ordering of past persons and events that renders them "significant". Auerbach observes that, for the Christian figural reader of the biblical text, God is both enactor and interpreter of the past persons and events depicted by the text: they have meaning and significance because they are the idiom in which God acts and speaks. Although one may refer to a figure "announcing" its fulfillment, it is ultimately God who does the announcing, for a person or an event is a *figura* precisely because it begins an extended divine utterance that embraces subsequent persons and events. "Figuralness" denotes the status of things as significant—not in themselves and not in their meanings—but insofar as they are, in all their concrete reality, the enacted intention of God to signify. If Jesus is the fulfillment of Joshua, that is because both Joshua and Jesus are moments within a single divine intention to signify. Discerning that intention as a literary congruence, the figural reader makes explicit the similarities by which otherwise separate events are related to one another as moments in a single, divine utterance.

As a consequence, figural interpretation is not, as Boyarin would have it, a matter of correlating linguistic representations with meanings, but rather of observing and describing a significant relationship between what might otherwise appear to be unrelated entities. When the figural interpreter describes that relationship, the description cannot be allowed to replace the graphic character of the representations being related. And by preserving the graphic character of the representations, the interpreter also leaves intact (or does not call into question) the historical reality of those persons and events that the text represents as God's performative utterance. From now on, I will use the term *figural*, as Auerbach does, to describe this relationship between representations and (implicitly) between those things that are represented. I will reserve the term *figurative*, on the other hand, for the correlation of a representation and its meaning, a meaning that is logically independent of the representation. "Logical independence" means that one can state the meaning apart from the representation without loss; the representation is, at best, a useful but dispensable illustration. When such a meaning is regarded as virtually identical with the representation, it is "literal"; when it is re-garded in opposition to the representation, it is "non-literal". The upshot of these distinctions is that the very possibility of *figurative* language is consti-tuted by the binary opposition between literality and non-literality; a *figural* relation, on the other hand, avoids entering into that opposition altogether.

We can now consider Auerbach's conception of figural reading in more detail by turning to his first example of it in his essay "Figura". The biblical verse at issue, Numbers 13:16, reads as follows: "Those were the names of the men whom Moses sent to scout the land [of Canaan]; but Moses changed the name of Hoshea son of Nun to Joshua." The second-century Church Father Tertullian reads this event figurally, focusing on Hoshea's new name, Joshua, of which the name Jesus is a contraction:

> For the first time [Hoshea] is called Jesus ... This ... was a figure of things to come. For inasmuch as Jesus Christ was to introduce a new people, that is to say us, who are born in the wilderness of this world, into the promised land flowing with milk and honey, that is to say, into the possession of eternal life, than which nothing is sweeter; and that, too, was not to come about through Moses, that is to say, through the discipline of the Law, but through Jesus, that is, through the grace of the gospel, our circumcision being performed by a knife of stone, that is to say, by Christ's precepts—for Christ is a rock; therefore that great man, who was prepared as a type of this sacrament, was even consecrated in figure with the Lord's name, and was called Jesus.[16]

Although one could understand Tertullian's comparisons non-literally (e.g., the physical land of Palestine as a figurative expression for the land of beatitude, or physical circumcision for spiritual obedience), Auerbach instead reads them as structural similarities between two patterns of past events that are themselves fully real. He underscores that reality by observing that although the event of Joshua's naming is a *figura*, Tertullian's representation of Joshua as a "prophetic annunciation" of Jesus does nothing to call into question the reality that Joshua would have possessed as an actual human being in his own right.[17]

Yet Auerbach recognizes that figural reading contains within itself, in the non-literal potential of its comparisons, the possibility of self-subversion.[18] And he can point to examples where, due to the vagueness of the structural similarities, the non-literal potential appears to gain the upper hand. Auerbach warns that Christian figural reading often "removed the thing told very far from its sensory base", forcing the reader "to turn his attention away from the sensory occurrence and toward its meaning." The danger here was that "the visual element of the occurrences might succumb under the dense texture of meanings";[19] all too often, he observes, "the sensory occurrence pales before the power of the figural meaning."[20] Auerbach explains how this supersession of sensory occurrence by meaning might come about. On the one hand, there is nothing non-literal in the accounts of Eve's creation in Genesis and the piercing of Jesus' side in the Gospel of John, taken by themselves: there is sleep, a rib, shaping, a piercing of flesh, water, blood. There is also a broad structural similarity between the two events: in both cases, a physical opening is made in the side of a male human being and something physical comes out of it (in one case, a rib; in the other, blood and water). Discerning this structural similarity, a figural reader might argue that the first physical event is a figural prophecy of the second, which is its fulfillment. But one could also go further and add what Auerbach calls a "doctrine" or "meaning", namely, that the mother of human beings "after the flesh" (Eve) is a literal description of the non-literal mother of human beings "after the spirit" (the Church). The more one becomes interested in this non-literal meaning, the less attention one will give to the literal, physical character of either figure or fulfillment.

Does Christian figural reading inevitably dissolve the sensory character of figure or fulfillment into non-sensory meanings? Unlike Boyarin, Auerbach does not regard dissolution as an inevitability but as an ever-present temptation to which Christianity often succumbed. The temptation is always there because, claims Auerbach, the figurative tension is built into the way Christians understand reality. The "antagonism between sensory appearance and meaning," he asserts, "permeates the early, and indeed the whole, Christian view of reality."[21] Christian figural interpretation avoided undermining itself insofar as figural readers understood the "spiritual" character of their readings to lie in their recognition of the figure's relationship to the fulfillment. The spiritual character did not reside in the subordination of a literal figure to a non-literal meaning that would, in the fashion of all binary oppositions, supersede or supplant it: "... in every case," writes Auerbach, "the only spiritual factor [in figural reading] is the understanding ... which recognises the figure in the fulfillment."[22] To recognize the figure in the fulfillment is a striking reversal of our usual habits of thought: rather than looking at the figure (Joshua) and seeing the fulfillment (Jesus), one looks at the fulfillment (Jesus) and sees *in him* the figure (Joshua).

And yet figural meaning often seems to seek independence from figural language; it seeks to dominate and ultimately supplant that of which it is the meaning. Meaning's power to undermine the reality of figure and fulfillment is not easy to resist: Auerbach observes that in many cases of figural interpretation, "what is perceived by the ... readers," he writes, "is weak as a sensory impression, and all one's attention is directed toward the context of meanings."[23] For Auerbach, the only way this force of meaning drained of sensory substance can be decisively resisted is by an absolute *kenôsis* or "emptying out" of meaning into fully realized, concrete imagery: but this will be the achievement not of interpretation but of poetic art. Figural interpretation constantly threatens to render meaning discarnate; Auerbach's *Mimesis* describes how figural art, beginning decisively with Dante's *Divine Comedy*, reversed this process and ushered in a Western tradition of secular literary realism. Dante's otherworldly fulfillment rendered his human characters so humanly real that they were thereby poised to claim their realism as wholly their own, independent of all otherworldliness. The larger plot of *Mimesis* describes how Christianity, in the wake of Dante, finally gave back to the world the concrete realism provisionally bequeathed to it by Judaism. From Boccaccio onward, this kind of concrete realism was made available apart from that spiritual, otherworldly fulfillment that Christians believed had constituted its very essence.

III

Auerbach argues that the reversal that Dante's poetry effected preserved humanistic realism, but at the expense of traditional Christian conceptions of the afterlife. The reversal turned on Dante's poetic handling of the figurative potential that Auerbach believed lurked within the Christian figural imagination. Boyarin, on the other hand, believes that the Christian figural imagination (at least in its Pauline form) is finally nothing but figurative: hence his explicit rejection of Auerbach's classic distinction between figural (or typological) reading and allegorical reading. This juxtaposition of Auerbach and Boyarin raises several questions: Does the very possibility of figurative (as opposed to figural) meaning reflect a fundamental misconception concerning the character of Christian interpretation—and even Christian identity? Would the reversal Auerbach describes even have been possible, let alone inevitable (as Boyarin suggests), if Christian interpreters had emphasized even more than did Auerbach the thoroughgoing priority of the figural over the figurative?

These questions are opened up in the work of Auerbach's foremost Christian theological reader, the late Hans Frei. In part, simply by virtue of his biography, Frei may have been unusually well-positioned to explore such questions. Born in Breslau, Germany, in 1922 into a non-observant Jewish family (whose name had, in an earlier generation, been shortened from Freiburg), Frei was baptized as an infant, for social and political reasons, into the Protestant State Church of Prussia. (In later years, he recalled with bemusement the consternation generated among family and friends by the fact that, in his case, the baptism had actually "taken".) When in 1934, the year after Faulhaber delivered his Advent sermons and the year before Auerbach emigrated to Turkey, it had become clear to Frei's parents that Christian baptism would offer no protection from the Nazi state to those of Jewish ancestry, Frei was sent at the age of twelve to a Quaker school in England. The entire family emigrated to the United States in 1938. Frei joined the Yale faculty in Religious Studies in 1957, the year Auerbach, Yale's Sterling Professor of Romance Languages, died.

Frei discovered in Auerbach's characterization of figural reading just that emphasis on the Bible's literal, narrative sense that he felt Christian readers of the Bible needed to recover if they were to rediscover Christianity's own essential identity. Yet Frei knew that the story of *figura* that Christians would need to tell must end differently from the story Auerbach had told in *Mimesis* . The turning point in Auerbach's story had been what he called the "eclipse of God" by humanity, signaled by Dante's poetry: the outcome was a purely secular humanism.[24] In contrast, Frei's own major work, *The Eclipse of Biblical Narrative*, would stay closer to the astronomical metaphor. For Frei, the eclipse marked an unfortunate but provisional interlude; for him as for the Christian tradition in general, authentic humanism could never be simply secular.[25] And yet, no less than Auerbach, Frei understood that any humanism constructed apart from the texts by which human beings fashioned their identities would finally become an anti-humanism. So the text—the narrative texts of Bible—would need to re-emerge from eclipse.

Frei's recourse to Auerbach denies both the Christian theological appropriateness and the practical inevitability of the binary oppositions Boyarin describes. At the same time, it sheds light on why such oppositions have been so prevalent in the Christian tradition. Yet Frei clearly diverges from Auerbach on the character of Christian identity at its origin. Frei insists that the identity of the religion is rooted in the identity of Jesus, a personal identity for which resurrection, if only as a plot development in the Gospels as literary narratives, is an essential ingredient.[26] But in the second chapter of *Mimesis*, we learn that for Auerbach, the resurrection is not constitutive of Jesus' identity; instead, "resurrection" is Peter's way of talking about the fresh *meaning* that he finds for *his own* life as a formerly unsteady follower of the humiliated and crucified Jesus. Or as one commentator on Auerbach put it, with a nice echo of 2 Corinthians 3:6: "Jesus dies, but Peter lives"—and therein, Frei might have observed, just insofar as Jesus' own resurrected *body* dissolves into the spiritual *meaning* of his life for others, does the possibility of subversion by non-literality first arise.[27] That possibility, Frei would suggest, follows directly from a failure to read the Gospels as literary narratives, for in the story as they tell it, Jesus dies, Jesus lives again—*and therefore* Peter lives.

Because Jesus lives, Peter can also live—*as Peter.* Peter lives his own life because, to invoke Paul's image, he is now a member of the body of Christ. But the body of Christ is irreducibly particular, uniquely Christ's own. How then does membership "in" that body enhance rather than suppress the individual identities of its members? Would it not make more sense for each of us to interpret the body of Christ as a metaphor for the various meanings that we might wish to give our own unique lives? Would not such "Christic meaning", precisely because it would no longer be attached to, and identified by, the actions and passions of that particular body, be sufficiently malleable to accommodate our own irreducible diversity? Conversely, if we all were to become identified by means of inclusion in Christ's body, in his person, would not our own uniqueness be superseded by Christ's? Would we not become hollow figures whose distinctiveness had given way to a single, universalizing fulfillment?

Frei argues otherwise. Jesus is the fulfillment of scriptural persons and events, but he fulfills them not by supplying a general meaning (the spiritual meaning that compensates for the letter's lack of meaning), but by supplying himself. In becoming ever more himself as the gospel narratives unfold, Jesus progressively detaches himself from what we now call "cultural constructions". He moves ever closer to an identification with the one he calls "Father", yet in doing so, becomes ever more himself, until, at the moment of resurrection, we see only the identity of Jesus in the Father's action by which he is raised. Maximal submission to the will of the Father coincides with maximal expression of individual identity. And as it is between Father and Son, so it is between the Son and his followers: whatever might be said about the similarity of followers to Jesus must coincide with Jesus' enhancement of their distinctively different identities. Frei makes this point while commenting on fictional literary characters presented as "Christ figures": "If such fiction is to remind us of Jesus and tell us his story over again, it must remind us by some other unique, particular person's or people's identity and story. And to do that means that in the very likeness of the mirrored story to the original, the concrete, specifying *difference* will have to stand out as clearly as the similarity, so that that other person will have his own individuality and not simply echo Jesus."[28] Although Frei's point concerns fictional Christ figures, he extends it to all human followers of Christ: "The particular story of Jesus, then, is pre-empted by him and him alone. Only those refractions of it will be credible and concrete that do not seek to reiterate it completely but only in part, not from too close by but at a distance, in the figure of a disciple rather than in the cosmic, miraculous, and abysmal destiny of the original."[29]

To rule out fictional representations or followers as "echoes" of Christ is to protect the unique identity of Christ. But the logic works the other way around as well: the follower's unique identity is also enhanced rather than absorbed and superseded. Because Jesus alone has his own identity, those who follow him have their own unique identities enhanced. Indeed, they thereby discover themselves to be just themselves and no one else: "Jesus does have an identity, and we have our identities in him"; or more precisely, "Jesus is he who is the way, the truth, and the life for men because he is these things in being the true Son of the Father, and thereby we also have identities";[30] "Because he has an identity, mankind has identity, each man in his particularity as the adopted brother of Jesus."[31] The implication for Jesus as the fulfillment of the prophecies of Israel is the same: "Jesus, at once as the manifestation of the presence of God acting and as the one who ... [has] a true identity of his own, can bestow it without distortion on the community of Israel in which he is a member."[32] In becoming who he is in all of his unsubstitutable individuality, Jesus has removed himself from the community and cultural constructions that formerly identified him, so that he might return to provide that community with his own identity, which is the self-identification and self-presentation of God:[33] "... his identity is so unsubstitutable now that he can bring it to bear as the identifying clue for the community which becomes focused through him. Indeed, the New Testament will ask just this of men: to identify themselves with the identity, not of a universal hero or savior figure, but of the particular person, Jesus of Nazareth, the manifest presence of God in their midst, who has identified himself with them."[34]

Now that Christ's identity is inalienably his own, there is no risk that the other's identity could ever be subsumed or supplanted by Christ's. There is no "sharing of identity" that could lay the groundwork for supersession; there is instead an "identifying with" that never dissolves into a "common identity". Human beings are invited to "identify with" one who, in his own unique identity, has chosen to "identify with" them. The very possibility of the action of "identifying with" presupposes the unsubstitutable and non-interchangeable identities of the agents. In the case of Israel—the community that is now invited to become "focused" through a Jesus whose identity is his alone and not any community's (Jewish or Christian)—the same requirement of unsubstitutable identity obtains. For the community does not abandon but rather enhances its own identity by identifying with the Jesus who has already identified himself with it. In a late essay, Frei made it unmistakably clear that Judaism and Christianity, "though closely intertwined, are quite distinct, each with its own integrity."[35] If Jesus Christ is the fulfillment of figures, then both Jews and Christians must equally be figures awaiting fulfillment. And because fulfillment means not the filling up of a glass only half-full, but the complete realization of unique and unsubstitutable identities, "fulfillment" in Christ has nothing whatever to do with a supersessionist relation between Christianity and Judaism, but everything to do with the willingness of individuals to give up false, self-serving identities for the sake of identifying themselves with God's own self-identification with them out of love.

Many of us think we understand well the threat posed by reading "according to the letter" alone, a threat we might characterize as "anti-humanistic fundamentalism". And many of us might be inclined to favor the common liberal-minded antidote to such cramped literalism, an antidote we might call "humanistic anti-fundamentalism"—the view that seeks out a common spirit and cheerfully tolerates different doctrines, but only as long as no one takes them too seriously. But I have been concerned in this essay with two possibilities that may be less obvious to us in our own cultural moment: an anti-literalism that is finally anti-human (which Boyarin warns us against), and a humanism that demands a certain kind of literalism (towards which Auerbach and Frei point). Reading according to the spirit *instead of* reading what is written obliterates the differences that constitute identity for the sake of achieving some pre-conceived sameness. But reading according to the spirit *by* reading what is written reveals that identity can never be based on sameness, that lives in common are not fashioned out of lives in general, and that who we really are can never be *less than* our visible, concrete, uniquely embodied selves (though we may be *more*—which suggests that doing full justice to what is written may compel one to say something further, but not something else, about spirit). But, as we have seen, this is a path fraught with danger: for it is very hard to say something further without saying something else.

Christianity demands respect for the letter of the spirit, respect for the grammars of difference that constitute identity. Christians choose to identify themselves with one who has already identified himself with each person, in all of that person's unsubstitutable uniqueness, a uniqueness that he enhances rather than suppresses. To what sort of practices should respect for the different grammars of identity lead Christians? As in learning a foreign language, here too, we would surely be led to learn the world's different grammars, to try to understand them as they are in their own right, perhaps one day even to employ them in ways that native users would recognize as properly idiomatic (even while our accents would continue to reveal our own differences from them). And while we were diligently learning the different grammars of identity in the hope of a commonality gained by mutual fluency, we would also begin to enact our lives together by means of mutual service. For mutual fluency is, so Christians affirm, a matter of eschatological hope; mutual service, on the other hand, is something that can happen right now. And in such service that respects the identities of others, it has been promised that we will discover our own.

NOTES

1 Cardinal Faulhaber, *Judaism, Christianity, and Germany*, trans. Rev. George D. Smith (New York, NY: Macmillan, 1935), p. 1.
2 Ibid., p. 2.
3 Ibid.
4 Ibid., p. 3.
5 Ibid., pp. 4–5.
6 Ibid., p. 8.
7 Ibid., p. 14.
8 Ibid.
9 Ibid., p. 107.
10 Ibid., p. 5.
11 Daniel Boyarin, *A Radical Jew: Paul and the Politics of Identity* (Berkeley and Los Angeles, CA: University of California Press, 1994).
12 For a study of Paul that emphasizes this continuity, see Richard B. Hays, *Echoes of Scripture in the Letters of Paul* (New Haven and London: Yale University Press, 1989). In *A Radical Jew*, Boyarin frequently takes issue with features of Hays' interpretation of Paul's biblical hermeneutic.
13 Erich Auerbach, "'Figura,'" trans. Ralph Manheim, *Scenes from the Drama of European Literature*, vol. 9 of Theory and History of Literature, eds. Wlad Godzich and Jochen Schulte-Sasse (Minneapolis, MN: University of Minnesota Press, 1984), pp. 11–76; Erich Auerbach, *Mimesis: The Representation of Reality in Western Literature*, trans. Willard R. Trask (Princeton, NJ: Princeton University Press, 1953).
14 "Epilegomena zu *Mimesis*," p. 10 n12, referred to by Jan M. Ziolkowski in his foreword to Erich Auerbach, *Literary Language and its Public in Late Antiquity and in the Middle Ages*, trans. Ralph Manheim (Princeton, NJ: Princeton University Press, 1965) p. x, n1.
15 I am, of course, restating Nietzsche's well-known illustration of the formation of concepts in his essay "On Truth and Lies in a Nonmoral Sense," in *Philosophy and Truth: Selections from Nietzsche's Notebooks of the Early 1870s*, trans. and ed. (with an introduction and notes), Daniel Breazeale (Atlantic Highlands, NJ: Humanities Press, 1979), p. 83.
16 Tertullian, as quoted by Auerbach, "'Figura,'" pp. 28–29.
17 Ibid., p. 29.
18 For a reading of *figura* in Auerbach that accentuates this side of his thought, see Timothy Bahti, *Allegories of History: Literary Historiography After Hegel* (Baltimore, MD: The Johns Hopkins University Press, 1992), chapter 5: "Auerbach's *Mimesis*: Figural Structure and Historical Narrative".
19 Auerbach, *Mimesis*, p. 48.
20 Ibid., p. 49.
21 Ibid.
22 Auerbach, "'Figura,'" p. 32.
23 Auerbach, *Mimesis*, p. 49.
24 Ibid., p. 202.
25 Hans W. Frei, *The Eclipse of Biblical Narrative: A Study in Eighteenth and Nineteenth Century Hermeneutics* (New Haven and London: Yale University Press, 1974).
26 Hans W. Frei, *The Identity of Jesus Christ: The Hermeneutical Bases of Dogmatic Theology* (Philadelphia, PA: Fortress Press, 1975).
27 Hans W. Frei, "Theological Reflections on the Accounts of Jesus' Death and Resurrection," in *Theology and Narrative: Selected Essays*, eds. George Hunsinger and William C. Placher (New York, NY: Oxford University Press, 1993), pp. 57–58.
28 Ibid., p. 56.
29 Ibid., p. 56. See David E. Demson, *Hans Frei and Karl Barth: Different Ways of Reading Scripture* (Grand Rapids, MI: Wm. B. Eerdmans Publishing Company, 1997), for the argument that Frei, in contrast to Barth, leaves out of his account of the New Testament depiction of Jesus' identity Jesus' gathering, upholding, and sending of the apostles. Demson writes that "Frei, by concentrating on Jesus' enacted identity in relation to God and on its manifestation by the act of God, but scarcely at all on Jesus' enacted identity in relation to the apostles and the confirmation of *that* identity by the act of God, leaves out of

account the apostles' identity—and ours, too, as participant in the apostles' identity" (p. 95). Rather than say that Frei's account leaves out the apostles' identity as well as the identities of subsequent followers, I think it more appropriate to say that because Frei is unwilling to risk formulations that might suggest some merger of Christ's identity with that of his followers, he is content to offer a purely formal specification of the way in which the individual identities of Christ's followers depend on their difference from Christ's identity for their own integrity as unique individuals. This formal specification of absolute difference coincides with a commonality between Christ and the follower that will nonetheless never dissolve into sameness. Absolute difference coincides with an absolute (i.e., self-emptying) divine "identifying with" and thereby resists any sort of shared identity.

30   Hans W. Frei, "Theological Reflections," p. 71.
31   Ibid., p. 81.
32   Ibid., p. 74.
33   Ibid., pp. 81–82.
34   Ibid., p. 86.
35   Hans W. Frei, "The 'Literal Reading' of Biblical Narrative in the Christian Tradition: Does It Stretch or Will It Break?" in *The Bible and the Narrative Tradition*, ed. Frank McConnell (New York, NY: Oxford University Press, 1986), p. 149.

IN DEFENSE OF ALLEGORY

ROBERT LOUIS WILKEN

'Where allegory and its variations, anagogy and the moral explanation appear, the understanding of the text is murdered.' So wrote Adalbert Merx in 1879 in his *Die Prophetie des Joel und ihre Ausleger.*[1] For generations now, biblical interpreters have scorned allegory, anagogy, tropology and all their works. Only the literal or historical sense, presented to us by the tools of historical criticism, can claim the allegiance of modern exegetes. I remember once when studying at Heidelberg in Germany discussing Origen's exegesis with Professor Hans Freiherr von Campenhausen. His only comment was: "Quatsch!" I am not sure how best to translate that into English, but I was certain, from the way von Campenhausen spit it out at me, that he had paid Origen no compliment.

In the twentieth century the hero of patristic exegesis has been Theodore of Mopsuestia who, it is thought, anticipated modern, i.e. correct methods of biblical interpretation. If Theodore had won the day, wrote Kendrik Grobel in *The Interpreter's Dictionary of the Bible* at the end of the 1950s, historical exegesis, which Grobel curiously identified with the Reformation, "might have emerged a thousand years earlier than it did." Grobel explains: "The now obvious answer that a passage of scripture, as of any other literature, has just one meaning unless there is exceptional indication of double meaning, far from being obvious, had to be won through the travail of many centuries."[2]

Obvious? Perhaps to a small circle of biblical critics! If there is anything that is obvious, it is that the notion of a single sense does not carry us very far in the interpretation of great works of literature, or of the Bible. I cite only one observation, a remark of Frank Kermode on the parables. "For the last century or so there has been something of a consensus among experts that parables of the kind found in the New Testament were always essentially simple, and always had the same kind of point, which would have been instantly taken by all listeners, outsiders included. Appearances to the

Robert Louis Wilken
Department of Religious Studies, University of Virginia, Charlottesville, VA 22903, USA

contrary are explained as consequences of a process of meddling with the originals that began at the earliest possible moment. The opinion that the parables must originally have been thus, and only thus, is maintained with an expense of learning I can't begin to emulate, against what seems obvious, that 'parable' does and did mean much more than that."[3]

Allegory has to do with words and things and events meaning "much more than that." Without being attentive to allegory, it is not possible to read the Bible. The term occurs only once, in Galatians 4, where St. Paul gives an allegorical interpretation of Abraham's two wives, Hagar and Sarah. "For it is written that Abraham had two sons, one by a slave and one by a free woman. But the son of the slave was born according to the flesh, the son of the free woman through promise. Now this is an *allegory:* these two women are two covenants. One is from Mount Sinai, bearing children for slavery; she is Hagar ... she corresponds to the present Jerusalem, for she is in slavery with her children. But the Jerusalem above is free, and she is our mother." (Gal 4:22–26; emphasis)

But the practice of allegory is well documented in the Scriptures. A good example from the Old Testament is the story told to King David by the prophet Nathan after David had Uriah the husband of Bathsheba killed by assigning him in front lines in the war against the Ammonites. What David did, writes the author of 2 Samuel, "displeased the Lord." (2 Sam. 11:26) Immediately afterward the Lord sent the prophet Nathan to David and Nathan told him the following story.

There once were two men in a certain city, one who was rich and the other poor. The rich man had many flocks and herds, but the poor man had only one little ewe lamb. The poor man brought up the ewe lamb along with his own children; it used to eat of his master's food and drink from his cup and it was like a daughter to him. One day a traveler came to the rich man and he wanted to prepare a feast for his guest. But he was unwilling to take one of the lambs from his own flock for the feast. So he took the poor man's lamb and prepared it for his guest. At this point in the story David broke in for he was very angry and said "As the Lord lives, the man who has done this deserves to die." Then Nathan says to David: "You are the man."

This story is an allegory. It speaks about one thing in terms of another. It is not a tale about a poor man and a ewe lamb, but a story to reprove David's sin. In its simplest form allegory is a device by which something—a person, a thing, an event, an animal—is made to refer to something in the moral or spiritual realm. Just as our interest perks up when someone begins to tell a story to make a point, so allegory gives pleasure by presenting one thing in the guise of something else. It gives me more pleasure, says Augustine, to contemplate the church as a woman with beautiful teeth (as in Song of Songs 4:2, "Your teeth are like a flock of shorn ewes ascending from the pool...") than to hear the same thing "without the support of the imagery."[4] By the use of concrete images allegory not only gives delight, it stirs our imagination to think in a fresh way about human behavior, moral principles or theological ideas. It is as fundamental to human thinking as the logical relations of numbers. As the literary critic C.S. Lewis wrote: "Allegory, in some sense, belongs not to medieval man but to man, or even to mind, in general. It is of the very nature of thought and language to represent what is immaterial in picturable terms."[5]

An example of the use of allegory in the New Testament is the parable of the sower. As crowds gathered about Jesus to hear him, he said: "A sower went out to sow. And as he sowed, some seeds fell along the path, and the birds came and devoured them. Other seeds fell on rocky ground where they had not much soil, and immediately they sprang up, since they had no depth of soil, but when the sun rose they were scorched; and since they had no root they withered away. Other seeds fell upon thorns, and the thorns grew up and choked them. Other seeds fell on good soil and brought forth grain, some a hundred fold, some sixty, some thirty. He who has ears, let him hear." (Matt 13:1–9)

Jesus is not instructing his hearers on how to sow seeds. The seed and the several types of soil are allegories to speak about the Word of God and the receptivity of different kinds of persons to the Word of God. For some the Word never enters the heart but like seed on a path is eaten by birds; others receive it like seed that falls among thorns; and still others give it a place where it can germinate like seed that falls in good soil. In the case of this parable Jesus not only uses allegory to teach, he explains the meaning of each of the details in the parable. For example, about the seed that falls among thorns he says: "As for what was sown among thorns, this is he who hears the word, but the cares of the world and the delight in riches choke the word, and it proves unfruitful." (Matt 13:22)

In the story of Nathan and the parable of the sower allegory is a self-conscious technique on the part of the speaker. Nathan intended his story to make David look at himself and at what he had done. But allegory is also used in the Scriptures as an interpretive device to discern a meaning that is not plainly given by the text. Besides Galatians 4, an example of this kind of interpretation can be found in Ephesians 5 where St. Paul in discussing marriage says: "Husbands should love their wives as their own bodies. He who loves his wife loves himself. For no man ever hates his own flesh, but nourishes and cherishes it, as Christ does the church, because we are members of his body." Then, he cites Genesis 2:24. "For this reason a man shall leave his father and mother and be joined to his wife, and the two shall become one flesh." Paul interprets the words of Genesis as follows: "This mystery is a profound one, and I am saying that it refers to Christ and the church ..." The passage in Genesis carries a double meaning, a sense other than what is plainly stated. At one level, it is speaking about the coming together of a man and woman in marriage and the love the husband has for the woman with whom he has been joined physically; but at another level, this union refers to the intimate bond that unites Christ with his church. In this passage Paul does not use the term allegory, but his approach to Genesis 1 is similar to his interpretation of Hagar and Sarah. He uses details in the text to uncover a truth that is deeper than what is given on the surface of the passage.

Another example from St. Paul is found in 1 Corinthians 10. There Paul is instructing the Corinthians how to live as a Christian community. His purpose is moral, to dissuade these new Christians from idolatry and immorality. Instead of simply saying, do not worship idols and citing the first commandment, "You shall have no other gods before me," St. Paul directs their attention to several biblical stories filled with images and lets the stories do his work for him. "I want you to know, brethren, that our fathers were all under the cloud, and all passed through the sea, and all were baptized into Moses in the cloud and in the sea, and all ate the same supernatural food and all drank the same supernatural drink. For they drank from the supernatural Rock which followed them, and the Rock was Christ." As in Ephesians, Paul gives these accounts a double meaning. He reports what the Scriptures record about God's relation to the Israelites in the desert, but he says that these events have another sense as well. They are speaking not only about deliverance through the sea and about being nourished by manna and water from a rock; they also are speaking about Baptism and the spiritual nourishment that comes from Christ. He concludes his discussion with the statement that these things were done "as types" (*typikos* in Greek, the Vulgate has *in figura*), as signs or examples to teach us how we are to live. These things, says Paul, were "written down for our instruction." (1 Cor. 10:11)

These three Pauline texts, Ephesians 5 and 1 Corinthians 10 and Galatians 4, provide a biblical foundation for the practice of allegory, i.e. that for Christians the Old Testament is to be read on more than one level. In the very first paragraph of his *Literal Commentary on Genesis*, Augustine cites Ephesians 5 and 1 Corinthians 10 to argue that the ancient narratives bear a "figurative meaning." "No Christian will dare say that the narrative [in the Old Testament] must not be taken in a figurative sense. For St. Paul says: 'Now all these things that happened to them were symbolic.' And he explains the statement in Genesis, 'And they shall be two in one flesh,' as a great mystery in reference to Christ and to the Church.'"[6] Origen of Alexandria, too, cites the same texts to refute Celsus's argument that the Bible "cannot be interpreted allegorically.'"[7]

It was St. Paul who taught the earliest Christian to use allegory. By giving us "some examples of interpretation," writes Origen, Paul showed us how to use allegory so that we "might note similar things in other passages.'"[8] Paul also pointed the way toward a rationale for the use of allegory. In 1 Corinthians he says that the things that took place in ancient times and are recorded in the Old Testament were "written for *our* instruction." That is, the meaning of what is written in the Bible is illuminated by looking at the later history that began with Christ. Its meaning cannot be restricted to what happened in the past. What a text says about past events and persons (things that *happened*, says Paul) is an integral part of what it means, but the task of interpretation is never exhausted by a historical account. The text belongs to a world that is not defined solely by its historical referent. For St. Paul this is not an enterprise in literary artifice, but a matter of divine revelation. Through Christ it is possible to discern a deeper meaning in the ancient events and to appropriate them "for our instruction." For the same Christ, "through whom are all things and through whom we exist"(1 Cor. 8:4), who was at work among the Israelites in the wilderness in ancient times, is alive and present in the Church today. This is the penetrating truth disclosed in the words, "and all ate the same spiritual food and all drank the same spiritual drink. For they drank from the supernatural Rock which followed them, and the Rock was Christ." (1 Cor. 10:4)

In its original sense, Christian allegory as an interpretive technique is a way of interpreting the Old Testament in light of the new things that have taken place with the coming of Christ. The New Testament does not need an allegorical interpretation because it speaks directly about Christ. For example, a passage such as "Christ our passover lamb is sacrificed for us" (1 Cor. 5:6) does not require another meaning than the meaning that is given in the passage itself. The spiritual meaning of the New Testament events is the literal meaning. The death and Resurrection of Christ do not point to something else; they are the mystery hidden before the ages; Christ is the paschal lamb. As a medieval exegete wrote: "Pro se [New Testament] stat sicut auditur; non est allegoria."[9] "The New Testament is to be interpreted as it is heard. It does not require allegory."

Allegory, then, is a term to refer to the "Christological" dimension of the Old Testament, what came to be called the "spiritual sense." Sometimes the term allegory is used to designate a particular method of rendering meaning, i.e. drawing a one-to-one relation between a thing, e.g. a seed, and the spiritual reality to which it refers, e.g. the Word of God. In this sense allegory is to be distinguished from other ways of discerning meaning, the moral or anagogical or typological. But in its more general sense allegory refers to the Christological meaning of the Old Testament. St. Jerome, the great biblical translator (and not so great commentator), said that the terms "allegory" and "spiritual sense" mean the same thing.[10] Gregory the Great said that the interpretation of the Scriptures is divided into the "historical" and the "allegorical" sense.[11] In Christian tradition there are only two senses, the plain sense, sometimes called the literal or historical sense (in the medieval distich, *littera gesta docet*, "the literal sense teaches us what happened"), and the Christological or spiritual sense, which can take different forms. The distinctive feature of allegory or the spiritual sense is that what happened in the Old Testament is viewed in light of what has come about through the death and Resurrection of Christ. In the words of a medieval thinker, Old

Testament passages are to be understood "non ex sensu quem faciunt, sed ex sensu quo fiunt," "not from the sense that is given but that which has come to be."[12]

Now it should be noted that allegory in this sense differs from the kind of allegory found in the Nathan story or the parable of the sower. In those passages allegory is given by the nature of the text. In the texts from 1 Corinthians and Galatians, however, St. Paul gives an allegorical interpretation of passages from the Old Testament whose meaning is *not* on the face of it allegorical. The story of the manna from heaven can be read as an account of God's gracious care for his people as they made their way from Egypt to the promised land *tout court*. Unlike the story of Nathan it does not require an allegorical interpretation. Yet the New Testament does give it an allegorical, i.e. Christological, interpretation and this meaning, when joined with other biblical passages, e.g. "bread from heaven", has shaped the Christian understanding of "manna" in the desert. For the Christian reader manna can never be seen simply as ordinary food. Likewise, the deliverance through the Red Sea can never be read simply as an account of the deliverance of the Israelites from slavery in Egypt; because of 1 Corinthians 10, and passages that speak of Christ as the passover lamb, the Exodus evokes for Christians the spiritual deliverance in Baptism.[13]

Not all Christian allegory is, however, derived from the New Testament. Early Christian interpreters soon extended the principles learned from St. Paul and other New Testament writers (e.g. John's reference to the bronze serpent in John 3:14 and to manna in John 6:31–34) to other passages from the Old Testament, for example, the sacrifice of Isaac in Genesis 22. So the question needs to be asked: on what basis does one give an allegorical interpretation of a passage when the Bible itself does not suggest such an interpretation? For example, is it legitimate to give an allegorical interpretation of the garments of the high priest in the book of Leviticus even though the New Testament does not suggest such an interpretation?[14] What of the book of Job? One of the greatest commentaries from Christian antiquity, Gregory the Great's *Moralia*, is a full blown allegorical exposition of the book of Job. Yet the significance of Job seems to lie in the theological and moral meanings that are explicitly set forth in the text. Why do Christian interpreters of the Old Testament insist that there is *more* to be found than is given by the plain sense?

Before proceeding further, however, let me bring forth some examples of early Christian exegesis. Too often contemporary discussion of hermeneutical questions does not move beyond theory. Yet it is only as one works with particular texts that it is possible to see the distinctive challenges that Christian interpreters faced (and face) and how they dealt with them. First, then, some illustrations after which we will return to the question I have just posed.

Isaiah 2:1–4: "The word which Isaiah the son of Amoz saw concerning Judah and Jerusalem. It shall come to pass in the latter days that the mountain of the house of the Lord shall be established as the highest of the mountains, and shall be raised above the hills; and all the nations shall flow to it, and many people shall come and say: 'come, let us go up to the mountain of the Lord, to the house of the God of Jacob …' For out of Zion shall go forth the law, and the word of the Lord from Jerusalem. He shall judge between the nations … and they shall beat their swords into plowshares … ; nation shall not lift up sword against nation, neither shall they learn war any more."

This is of course one of the most familiar passages in the book of Isaiah. It is used as a canticle in morning prayer in the daily Office. The key to the interpretation of this passage is the phrase "in the latter days", which is alluded to in several places in the New Testament, notably Hebrews 1: "In many and various ways God spoke of old to our fathers by the prophets; but *in these last days* he has spoken to us by a Son, whom he appointed the heir of all things."[15] Early Christian commentators noted that the phrase "in the last days", also occurs in Acts 2:17 (inserted into a citation of Joel 2:28–32) to refer to the outpouring of the Holy Spirit.

According to Cyril of Alexandria, the "time" to which the prophet refers is an age in which the power of evil will be overcome "not in one country and city … but in every place under the heavens." This, in the view of Christian interpreters, can only refer to the coming of Christ and the spread of the Church. "This oracle," writes Cyril, "has been accomplished among those who were on earth in the last days, i.e. at the last times of the present age, in which the only begotten son of God the Word shined forth, born of a woman. … Christ showed forth the church of the nations, as it were in the last time, that is at the end of this age (Heb. 9:26)." (*Patrologia Graeca* 70, 68c). In this interpretation the verse, "For out of Zion shall go forth the law, and the word of the Lord from Jerusalem" refers to the preaching of the Gospel in Jerusalem that brought into being the Church that spread throughout the world.

The starting point for such a Christological and ecclesiological interpretation of prophetic oracles is that the words of the prophets have been fulfilled. It is this to which the New Testament bears witness. "Today this scripture has been fulfilled in your hearing." (Luke 4:21) In his commentary on Micah 4, the parallel to the oracle in Isaiah 2, Cyril cites St. Paul's words, "In Christ there is a new creation, the old has passed away."[16] This means, says Cyril, that Christ refashions for us a new way that was unknown to those in former times. No longer can the words and stories of ancient times refer solely to national or political events or to "sensible" things. We do not, writes Cyril, flee "Egyptian taskmasters but the tyranny of unbelief" and "we eat the spiritual manna and the bread from heaven." And then he adds, choosing his words carefully, when the ancient texts speak "historically" their words must be "taken in another sense," i.e. allegorically.[17] In ancient times things meant one thing, now they mean something else. "Aliter tunc … aliter nunc,"[18] as one medieval writer put it.

For the Christian interpreter Christ is the chief content of the Bible. As Henri de Lubac puts it in his magisterial work on the Christian exegetical tradition: "Jesus Christ gives unity to the Scriptures because he is its end and fulness. Everything in it relates to him. He is finally its only object. He is, one might say, the whole of exegesis."[19] The Bible is a book that directs us to Jesus Christ, "the same yesterday and today and forever" (Heb. 13:8) but always through the temporal and historical. Again Cyril: "The *skopos* of the inspired Scripture is the mystery of Christ signified to us through a myriad of different kinds of things. Someone might liken it to a glittering and magnificent city, having not one image of the king, but many, and publicly displayed in every corner of the city ... Its aim, however, is not to provide us an account of the lives of the saints of old. Far from that. Rather its *skopos* is to give us knowledge of the mystery [of Christ] through those things by which the word about him might become clear and true."[20]

Now to a quite different kind of text, *Song of Songs 4:12–15:* "A garden locked is my sister, my bride, a garden locked, a fountain sealed. Your shoots are an orchard of pomegranates with all choicest fruits, henna with nard, nard and saffron, calamus and cinnamon, with all tress of frankincense, myrrh and aloes, with all chief spices–a garden fountain, a well of living water, and flowing streams from Lebanon."

The phrase that is of interest in this passage is "living water." This image is of course familiar to readers of the Bible. It occurs in Jeremiah 2:13, "they have forsaken me, the fountain of living water," in Zechariah 14:8, and in John 4:10 in Jesus's discourse with the Samaritan woman. The phrase is capable of differing interpretations, and in its original setting within the Song it is crowded in with a number of other images. In the context of Song 4 it appears relatively innocuous. The only thing that might imply a more exalted interpretation, observes a modern commentator, is that the next phrase, "flowing streams from Lebanon," suggests "a kind of superlative expression for the best water, such as that which would have come from the heights in the Spring."[21]

In his homilies on the Song of Songs, Gregory of Nyssa takes "living waters" to be an image of the divine life which is "lifegiving" (*zoopoios*). He writes: "We are familiar with these descriptions of the divine essence as a source of life from the Holy Scriptures. Thus the prophet, speaking in the person of God, says: 'They have forsaken me, the fountain of living water' (Jer. 2:13). And again, the Lord says to the Samaritan woman: 'If you knew the gift of God, and who it is that is saying to you, "Give me a drink," you would have asked him, and he would have given you living water." (John 4:10) And again he says: 'If any one thirst, let him come to me and drink. He who believes in me, as the Scripture has said, 'Out of his heart shall flow rivers of living water.' Now this he said about the Spirit, which those who believed in him were to receive.'" (John 7:38–39)

"Here in all these places by 'living water' is meant the divine nature. So too in our text the infallible Word declares that the bride is a well of living waters that have flowed down from Lebanon. Now here is a very strange paradox. All wells hold still water; only in the bride is there said to be running water. She has the depth of a well together with the constant flow of a river. Now how can we really do justice to the wonders revealed here in the symbol that is applied to the bride? It would seem that she has no further height to reach now that she has been absolutely compared to the very archetype of all beauty. Very closely does she imitate his source in her own, his life in hers, that living water by hers. God's Word has life, and so too does the soul that receives him. And this water flows from God, as he the source, explained when he said, 'From God I proceeded and came' (John 8:42). And the bride embraces and holds what flows into the well of her soul, and thus she becomes a storehouse of that living water that flows, or rather, rushes down from Lebanon, as the Word tells us."[22]

Gregory's interpretation of Song 4:15 is inspired by the use of a similar image in Jeremiah 2 and John 4, as well as other biblical texts about living water. In a later homily, he returns to the image of lifegiving water, but now he is thinking of the "spring" in Genesis 2:6 (LXX) that watered the face of the earth. "As you came near the spring you would marvel, seeing that the water was endless, as it constantly gushed up and poured forth. Yet you could never say that you had seen all the water." Gregory compares looking at the spring to "fixing one's gaze on the infinite beauty of God. It is constantly being discovered anew, and it is always seen as something new and strange in comparison with what the mind had already understood. As God continued to reveal himself, man continues to wonder, and never exhausts his desire to see more, since what one is waiting for is always more magnificent, more divine, than all that one has already seen."[23]

Gregory was well aware that there were other images to express the nature of God. Plotinus, for example, had used expressions such as "inexhaustible infinity," or "boiling over with life" for the divine.[24] One can speak of God as the source of life without using the language of the Bible. The point is not that "living water" expresses things better than "inexhaustible infinite" or "boiling over with life." The significance of the phrase is that it is found in the Bible and carries overtones drawn from Biblical narrative of God's self-disclosure.

Images such as "living water" hold a privileged place in Christian discourse and one of the tasks of Biblical interpretation is to keep that place secure. They are not, as Janet Martin Soskice observes, simple metaphors; they are "almost emblematic." The meanings associated with them cannot be disengaged from God's revelation in Israel and in Christ as well as its reception by the Church. "A favoured model continues to be so in virtue of its own applicability certainly, but also because the history of its application makes it already freighted with meaning."[25] Metaphors and images and symbols drawn from elsewhere, no matter how apt, have a wholly different impact on the Christian imagination. Like rhetorical ornaments that momentarily delight the hearer, they are ephemeral and are soon forgotten.

Allegory is about privileging the Biblical language. The words and images, the events and persons of the Bible make a greater claim on us than any other language or history or persons. The allegorical interpretation of the Bible assumes that it is better to express things in the language of the Bible than to draw one's language and imagery from elsewhere. Because certain words or images or events are found in the Bible, they carry overtones of things that are spoken of elsewhere in the Bible. One need not use the language of the psalms to pray, but by using the psalms one moves in a world defined by Jerusalem and Mt. Zion, the deliverance from Egypt, the exile in Babylonia, the Law, God as King, sacrifices in the temple, as well as the Christian mysteries, e.g. Christ's baptism (Ps. 2), passion (Ps. 22), Resurrection (Ps. 8), or Ascension (Ps. 68). In the same way, Christian exegesis listens for echoes that reverberate from elsewhere in the Scriptures.

I can illustrate this point by one tradition of interpretation of Genesis 1:26: "Then God said, 'Let us make man in our image, after our likeness ...'" In his commentary on Genesis, Didymus the Blind, a late fourth century Christian thinker, first gives the conventional interpretation of the text, that the phrase "image of God" means that "man is a reasonable creature." But then he notes that the text has a second term, "likeness." This term reminds him of 1 John 3 where it is said that when God "appears we shall be *like* him." Didymus writes: "One should also observe that God speaks of two kinds of becoming. 'Let us make man according to our image and likeness.' I think that an exact correspondence without any difference is characteristic of 'likeness,' in the sense that likeness is the highest degree of image, while the image cannot be said to be precisely like the model in all respects as is the case with the likeness. Image would be a beginning and a prologue to the likeness."

What this means, says Didymus, is that we are first made in God's image, and only later do we become his "likeness." By advancing to perfection the image becomes the likeness of God, which St. John sets forth when he writes: 'Beloved we are God's children now, it does not yet appear what we shall be, but we know that when he appears we shall be *like* (*omoioi*). (1 John 3:2) We are already made according to the image of God and we hope to become according to the likeness."[26]

To Christian interpreters the term "likeness" (*omoiosis*) suggested that Genesis 1:26 is not simply speaking about creation, what Hugh of St. Victor called God's first work, the work of foundation; but also refers to God's second work, the work of redemption. Image of God was seen as the state in which human beings were created, and likeness to God as the state into which they were transformed by conforming to the image of Christ. By interpreting "likeness" as that to which we aspire, Didymus is able to give the text a Christological interpretation. Restoration is not a return to a prior state—it is the acquiring of something new, the image of Christ. In the words of St. Paul: "We all, with unveiled face, beholding the glory of the Lord, are being changed into his likeness from one degree of glory to another ..." (2 Cor. 3:18)

Now to return to the question of why Christian interpreters always insist on more than the plain sense in reading the Old Testament. I want to consider one more example from patristic exegesis. The Biblical text is Psalm 73:25–28 and the interpreter is St. Augustine. "Whom have I in heaven but thee? And there is nothing upon earth that I desire besides thee. My flesh and my heart may fail, but God is the strength of my heart and my portion for ever. For lo, those who are far from thee shall perish; thou dost put an end to those who are false to thee. But for me it is good to be near God; I have made the Lord God my refuge, that I may tell of all thy works."

The phrase I want to focus on is, "for me it is good to cleave to God" (in Augustine's Latin, "mihi adhaerere Deo bonum est"). Indeed, one might argue that "cleaving to God" is at the center of the Biblical tradition, for it is the end toward which our lives are directed. That is surely the way the Bible was understood by the church fathers. The point of the Incarnation, God's gracious descent into human life and history was, as Origen put it, that human beings, by knowing God in the flesh, might have "fellowship with him through Christ", (*Contra Celsum* 4:6) i.e. cleave to God.

Augustine interprets Ps. 73:28 in light of God's promise in the book of Leviticus that if the people of Israel keep his commandments "I will walk among you, and will be your God, and you shall be my people." (Lev. 26:12) The connection between this passage in Leviticus and Christ is already made in 2 Cor. 6:16–7:1 where St. Paul had cited it to show that there was no partnership between righteousness and iniquity, nor fellowship between light and darkness. Therefore, he exhorted the Corinthians, "make holiness perfect in the fear of God." Augustine writes: "This passage ("I will be their God") is the reward of which the psalmist speaks in his prayer, 'For me to cleave to God is good.' ... There can be no better good, no happier happiness than this: life for God, life from God, who is the well of life, in whose light we shall see light. Of that life the Lord himself says, 'This is life eternal, that they may know you the one true God, and Jesus Christ whom you have sent'... This is his own promise to his lovers: 'He that loves me keeps my commandments; and he that loves me is loved of my Father and I will love him and will show myself to him."[27]

For Augustine Ps. 73:28 invites a Trinitarian exposition because it is only through the outpouring of the Holy Spirit that humans are able to love God, that is, cleave to God. To support this interpretation, he cites Rom. 5:5: "God's love has been poured into our hearts through the Holy Spirit which has been given to us." Augustine takes love here to refer to love toward God (not God's love for us) for it is through love, given by the Holy Spirit, that we are joined to God. Man not only receives instruction as to how we are to love (through the commandments), but "he also receives the Holy Spirit, whereby there arises in his soul the delight in and the love of God, the supreme and changeless Good. It is his here and now, while he walks by faith, not yet by sight; that having this as earnest of God's free bounty, he may be fired in heart to 'cleave' to his Creator, kindled in mind to come with the shining of the true light; and thus receive from the source of his being the only real well-being." (Ibid., 5.3).

What then is the 'more' that is found in the Old Testament by Christian interpreters, the layer of meaning that is present though seldom explicit? The unanimous testimony of the early Church is that the God disclosed in Jesus Christ and the sending of the Holy Spirit is the God revealed in the Scriptures as a whole. This is why it is possible for St. Augustine to interpret the words of the psalm, "it is good for me to cleave to God" in light of the mystery of the Holy Trinity. It is not enough to discern the meaning of the word "cleave" in Biblical Hebrew, or to construct the historical setting in which the psalm was written. If Psalm 73 was written "for our instruction", it must be interpreted in light of what is known of God through the revelation in Christ and the sending of the Holy Spirit. One can no longer speak about "cleaving to God" without acknowledging that it is through the gift of the Holy Spirit that we are able to love God.

The Biblical image that best expressed this understanding was the scroll of Ezekiel 2:9–10 that had "writing on the front and on the back." (also Rev. 5:1) In the Latin Vulgate "front" and "back" were translated "intus" and "foris," inside and outside. It was this "inner" and "outer" that shaped the dialectic of Biblical interpretation. Again and again the church fathers speak of moving from the outer sense, the surface meaning, to a deeper inner understanding of the text. This inner sense is not archane or esoteric, it is the sense given by the Holy Spirit who bears witness to Christ. It is only through the Spirit that one comes to know Christ and only through Christ that one is able to understand the Scriptures. John Chrysostom: "You see, there is not even a syllable or even one letter contained in Scripture which does not have great treasure concealed in its depths. Hence, we must be guided by grace from above and accept the enlightenment of the Holy Spirit, and only then approach the divine sayings. That is, Sacred Scripture does not call into play human wisdom for the understanding of its writings, but the revelation of the Spirit, so that we may learn the true meaning of its contents and draw from it great benefit."[28] It is apparent, then, that the historical study of the text, i.e. its background and setting, can only be preparatory to the task of interpretation. It is the necessary spadework, like looking up words in a dictionary, but it can never be sufficient. The real work of interpretation comes as the interpreter relates the text to what it reveals to us of the Triune God and, one might add, of ourselves.

There is a sense in which the Bible of the Christians is a different book from the writings that come down to us from the ancient Near East. Christians did not rewrite the Old Testament to suit Christian taste, but they read it in a Greek translation and the early Latin translation was based on the Greek. One might argue that the Christian Bible is not the Hebrew Bible but the Greek Bible of the early Church. The interpretation that took form in the early centuries was based on the Greek Old Testament, the Septuagint, not the Hebrew text. This Bible, when read in conjunction with the Greek New Testament, shaded the meaning of words, highlighted certain images, and privileged certain persons or events. In short, the book carried by the Christian community and read in light of its practices and beliefs had its own distinctive character. In this Bible the term "likeness" in Genesis 1 took on a depth of meaning that was not present in the Old Testament itself, and the "living waters" was now read with eyes attuned to the Gospel of John. As men and women lived by it, lectors read it and bishops preached on it, the faithful prayed it, and theologians debated its meaning, they discovered a spiritual world that was drawn from the books of the ancient Near East but was not identical with it. It is with this book that Christian exegesis must begin.

Another way of putting this is to say that there is no interpretation of the Bible without commentary. The first and most important commentary was of course the New Testament, but this was complemented by the creeds and Liturgy and Christian practices. Against the gnostics, Irenaeus argued that the Bible was unintelligible without reference to the teaching about the one God and the incarnate Christ sent from God as expressed in the rule of faith, the early creedal formulas that were the basis of the Apostles Creed. Against the detractors of the Holy Spirit, Basil of Caesarea argued for the divinity of the Holy Spirit by referring to the baptismal formula, "I baptize you in the name of the Father and of the Son and of the Holy Spirit." The Bible is to be interpreted not simply in light of its original context or setting, i.e. those factors that contributed to the language, concepts and form of the text; it must also be seen in light of what comes from the Bible.

Historical criticism has been so preoccupied with what came before and existed at the time of composition that it has ignored what came afterward, what came into being as a result of the events that took place and the text of the Bible itself. Context needs to be understood to embrace the Church, its liturgy, its way of life, its practices and institutions, its ideas and beliefs. Without the Bible these things would not have come into being, and without the Church and its life as a commentary the Bible is a sealed book for Christians.

Within the Church's tradition certain words and images came to be associated with others, an event or a person came to take on deeper and more paradigmatic sense than was evident before the coming of Christ (for example, Paul's discussion of Adam in Romans 5). When Gregory of Nyssa interprets the life-giving water as a reference to God, he is not striking out on his own; he is working within a tradition of interpretation. To the modern reader, patristic allegory often appears capricious and arbitrary, yet as our examples have shown there is always a verbal key to any given interpretation, and interpretation is disciplined by the Church's teaching and practice. And one must not forget that not every interpretation was received. Only what was plausible in light of the Scriptures as a whole took hold in the life of the Church. Like any image or figure or line in a poem, allegory enlightened only as it was loved and remembered.

The reason a strictly historical approach to the Bible, i.e. an interpretation without commentary, is inadequate is that it is incapable of synthesizing what the Bible says as Bible, i.e. as the book of the Church. It can offer various kinds of syntheses, e.g. a cultural history of the ancient Near East, a chapter in the religious history of the Roman world, to mention the most obvious. But what it cannot offer is an interpretation of the Bible as a book about the Bible's proper subject, the Triune God, creator and redeemer. The "subject matter" of the Scriptures, wrote Hugh of St. Victor in the 11th century, is the work of creation and redemption. "For there are two works in which all that has been done is contained. The first is the work of foundation; the second is the work of restoration. The work of foundation is that whereby those things which were not came into being. The work of restoration is that whereby those things which had been impaired were made better. Therefore, the work of foundation is the creation of the world with all its elements. The work of restoration is the Incarnation of the Word with all its sacraments, both those which have gone before from the beginning of time, and those which come after, even to the end of the world."[29]

For most of the Church's history theology and Scriptural interpretation were one. Theology was called *sacra pagina* and the task of interpreting the Bible was a theological enterprise. The Church's faith and life were seen as continuous with the Biblical narrative, and the Scriptures were interpreted within the context of a living theological and spiritual tradition. Even the Reformation appeal to "sola scriptura" assumed that the Bible was the book of the Church and that its interpretation was to be shaped by the Church's faith. In recent years, however, biblical scholarship has become a world to itself, divorced from the Church's theological and spiritual traditions. With the emergence of new historical disciplines in the 18th century and the application of these disciplines to the Scriptures, scholars began, unwittingly at first, to construct a new context in which to place the Scriptures. Up to that time the Bible was read as a book that spoke of the things of Christian faith and was interpreted within the framework of the Church's faith and practice. Historical criticism worked with the assumption that if the Scripture was understood in its original setting, it would be possible to understand more fully the revelation contained in the Bible. But over time the study of the Bible was disengaged from Christian tradition.

The more the Bible was studied historically, the more it came to appear foreign to Christian faith and life, a book whose home was the ancient world. It was taken as axiomatic that the scholarly study of the Bible had to exclude references to Christian teaching, for example, as reflected in the writings of the church fathers or in the decrees of the ancient councils. The notion that the Nicene Creed might play a role in understanding the Biblical conception of God, for instance, appeared ludicrous. As a consequence,

Biblical scholarship acquired a life of its own as a historical enterprise independent of the Church (and of the synagogue). Today its home is the university. The other Bible, the Bible of the Church, is, however, alive, and people live (and die) by it. The Church's interpretation is embedded in the liturgy, in the catechetical tradition, in patristic, medieval and reformation theological writings, in spiritual and devotional works, in hymns, and—let us not forget—in the Bible itself. The Christian interpretation of Psalm 22 and Isaiah 53 begins in the New Testament.

The great accomplishment of the Christian exegetical tradition was that it offered a comprehensive understanding of the Bible as Holy Scripture. In its pages the fulness of Christian faith and life could be found in bewildering detail and infinite variety. That we should find ourselves intrigued by this synthesis does not mean that the exegesis of the middle ages should be restored without being filtered through our experience and thinking, but it does mean that the traditional spiritual interpretation offers us a vision of what a genuine synthesis should look like. And in our riven and fragmented theological world that is a gift to be cherished. As John Henry Newman wrote: "In all ages of the Church, her teachers have shown a disinclination to confine themselves to the mere literal interpretation of Scripture … It may almost be laid down as an historical fact, that the mystical [i.e. spiritual] interpretation and orthodoxy will stand or fall together."[30]

NOTES

1 *Die Prophetie des Joel und ihre Ausleger von den ältesten Zeiten bis zu den Reformatoren: eine exegetisch-kritisch und hermeneutisch* (Verlag des Buchh. des Waisenhauses, 1879), p. 112.
2 *The Interpreter's Dictionary of the Bible*, Vol. 2 (New York, NY: 1962), p. 719.
3 *The Genesis of Secrecy: On the Interpretation of Narrative* (Cambridge, MA: Harvard University Press, 1979), p. 25.
4 *De Doctrina Christiana* 2.11–13.
5 C. S. Lewis, *The Allegory of Love: A Study in Medieval Tradition* (London: Oxford University Press, 1958), p. 45.
6 *De Genesi ad litteram* 1.1.
7 *Contra Celsum* 4.49.
8 *Hom. in Gen.* 5.1.
9 Henri de Lubac, *Éxégèse Médiévale. Les quatre sens de l'Écriture* (Paris: Aubier 1964), Vol. 4, p. 11.
10 *In Amos* 1.2.4 (*PL* 25, 1027d).
11 *In Hiezech.* 1.2.1.
12 Raoul Ardent, *Hom. in dom. 12 post. Trin.* (*Patrologia Latina* 155, 2035d).
13 Tertullian, *De Baptismo* 9.
14 See Origen, *Hom. in Levit.* 6.1ff.
15 See also Hebrews 9:26, "he appeared once for all *at the end of the age.*" Emphasis added.
16 *Comm. in Micah* 4.1–3 (Pusey 1:657 and 662).
17 *Patrologia Latina* 91, 1186a.
18 Rabanus Maurus, *In Num.* 3.13 (*Patrologia Latina* 108, 631a).
19 *Éxégèse Médiévale. Les quatre sense de l'Écriture* (Paris: Aubier 1959), Vol. 1, p. 322.
20 *Patrologia Latina* 69, 308c.
21 Roland Murphy, *The Song of Songs* (Minneapolis, MN: Fortress Press, 1990), p. 157.

22   Gregory of Nyssa, *Hom. in Cant. 9* Hermannus Langerbeck, ed. *Gregorii Nysseni In Canticum Canticorum edidit* ... (Leiden: E. J. Brill, 1960), pp. 292–293.
23   Gregory of Nyssa, *Hom. 11 in Cant. 5.2* Ibid., p. 321.
24   Plotinus, *Enneads* 6.5.12.
25   Janet Martin Soskice, *Metaphor and Religious Language* (Oxford: Clarendon Press, 1985) p. 158.
26   *Didyme l'Aveugle. Sur La Genèse.* Eds. Pierre Nautin and Louis Doutreleau (Sources Chrétiennes, No. 233: Paris: Iditions due Cerf, 1976), 1:146–150.
27   *De spiritu et littera* 37.22.
28   Chrysostom, *Hom. in* Gen. 21.1.
29   *On the Sacraments of the Christian Faith.* Trans. Roy J. Deferrari (Cambridge, MA: Medieval Academy of America, 1951), Prologue 2, p. 3.
30   *The Arians of the Fourth Century* (London: Rivington, 1833), pp. 104–105.

"WE ARE COMPANIONS OF THE PATRIARCHS" OR SCRIPTURE ABSORBS CALVIN'S WORLD[1]

KATHRYN GREENE-McCREIGHT

Among readers of the Bible influenced by the "Yale school" of narrative theology, it has become commonplace to speak of scripture "absorbing the world" of the reader.[2] George Lindbeck uses the metaphor to describe his cultural-linguistic model of construing doctrine which creates the possibility of post-liberal, intratextual theology: "Intratextual theology redescribes reality with the scriptural framework rather than translating scripture into extrascriptural categories. It is the text, so to speak, which absorbs the world, rather than the world the text."[3] Lindbeck's remarks about intratextual theology are influenced by Hans Frei's observation that the direction of pre-critical interpretation "was that of incorporating extra-biblical thought, experience, and reality into the one real world detailed and made accessible by the biblical story—not the reverse."[4] Frei and Lindbeck both are influenced by their Yale colleague, William Christian, whose work had cleared the way for them to critique the reversal of the direction of biblical interpretation: a reversal which is, in their view, the troll under the bridge of modern theology. Bruce Marshall, a student of both Frei and Lindbeck, has in his turn explored the metaphor of the narrative reader's Bible "absorbing the world" to see whether "it might be the heart of an adequate and plausible response to the question about whether Christian beliefs are true."[5]

While these scholars understand the Bible's absorption of the world to be a key feature of a post-liberal biblical hermeneutics, none of them tells us in concrete terms what such an absorption would actually entail. What would "absorptive exegesis" look like? What would our world look like if it indeed were absorbed into the biblical world? Would this mean that asses

Kathryn Greene-McCreight
198 McKinley Avenue, New Haven, CT 06515, USA

could speak to their riders, that grown men could walk on the sea like huge water-bugs, that prayers readily could heal youths who had fallen sermon-sleepily out of second storey windows? Maybe so, maybe not, depending on the example and on the reader. More importantly, the claim that Scripture absorbs the world of the narrative reader entails a prior claim that the reader is one with, and fully present to, the characters whose stories are read in the pages of the Bible. This in turn entails a yet prior nest of theological assumptions about the biblical text and its Divine Author.[6] It is the conjunction of this nest of assumptions (generally referred to under the term "the rule of faith") with an *ad hoc* use of a whole array of interpretive practices which render exegesis "absorptive".

Hans Frei pointed to the Genevan Reformer, John Calvin, as one of the pre-critical interpreters who read the Bible as one continuous narrative, whose reality was overcome by the reality of the biblical world.[7] The description which George Lindbeck gives of classical hermeneutics can be illustrated easily with Calvin, for Calvin clearly does read the Bible as "a canonically and narrationally unified and internally glossed (that is, self-referential and self-interpreting) whole centered on Jesus Christ, and telling the story of the dealings of the Triune God with his people and his world in ways which are typologically ... applicable to the present."[8] Therefore, we can illustrate what this world-absorptive capacity of the narrative reader's Bible looks like in exegetical practice by considering Calvin's biblical interpretation.

One of the many places in Calvin's exegesis in which this absorptive character of the Bible becomes clear is in the discussion which prefaces his commentary on Genesis, and in the way in which this discussion plays out in the ensuing commentary. This section of the commentary, a commonplace often referred to as "the Argument", sets forth and summarizes the main themes of the biblical book at hand. In the modern period, of course, the practice of introducing a commentary with the "argument" of the book to be discussed has for the most part been abandoned. The practice assumes that biblical books bear a thematic unity. Historical-critical methods in general seek, if not explicitly to reject such a notion of biblical unity, at the very least to set it aside in reading the biblical texts.

However, if we were to consider the nest of theological assumptions which lies behind Calvin's "argument" sections, we might gain insight into some important elements of pre-critical interpretation, not only how Scripture absorbs the world, but other aspects as well which may now seem mysteriously veiled to us. For example, in the "Argument" which opens Calvin's commentary on Genesis, we find that the conviction regarding the unity of God and its corollary, formal canonical unity, calls for "ad hoc" applications of figural exegesis in the ensuing commentary. This is true even while Calvin insists that he is searching for the plain and simple sense of the text of Scripture. It is this tool of figural exegesis, working in conjunction with classical theological assumptions regarding the biblical text and its Divine

Author normed by the rule of faith, much as indicated in Lindbeck's description, which results in Scripture's capacity to absorb the interpreter's world.

But how does this actually happen? First of all, Calvin reads Genesis itself as both an episode within and a summary or proleptic vision of the "Gospel story" as a whole. The story of Genesis is read not only as the "history of the creation of the world" as Calvin calls it, a story about long ago and far away, but also as the sum content of the Christian story itself. Because it is the sum of the Christian story, it thereby automatically *is* the story of the reader, a story which is recapitulated daily in the life of the Christian. Thus Calvin says at the end of his "Argument":

> We are companions of the patriarchs; for since they possessed Christ as the pledge of their salvation when he had not yet appeared, so we retain the God who formerly manifested himself to them.[9]

How odd, one might react, that Calvin understands Genesis to tell the Christian story, thereby rendering us companions of the Patriarchs. It is easy to imagine how Calvin could understand the oneness of the community of faith throughout time such that we, even now, are companions of the Patriarchs. But how can Genesis incorporate the Gospel of Jesus Christ and the founding of the Church? Surely Calvin cannot mean that the stories of these happenings are read in the pages of the first book of Torah. Yet this is exactly what Calvin does mean.

The purpose of Moses, says Calvin, in beginning the book of Genesis with the creation accounts, is "to render God, as it were, visible to us in his works." Calvin says that God, otherwise invisible, here "clothes himself, so to speak, with the image of the world, in which he would present himself to our contemplation." He then goes on to say, following Paul's letter to the Romans, that while God invites us to himself by means of the created order, this serves only to leave us without excuse, for natural knowledge of God is not "sufficient for salvation". Therefore, God has added a "new remedy", which is, interestingly enough according to Calvin, not Jesus but Scripture, and specifically the Torah: "For if the mute instruction of the heaven and the earth were sufficient, the teaching of Moses would have been superfluous."

After eight pages (in King's translation of the commentary), Calvin finally lays out what he understands to be the "argument" or plot of the book of Genesis, which, we remember, he has indicated is the Christian story. It runs like this: 1) after the world is created, humankind is placed in it, that beholding the works of God, all might reverently adore their Author; 2) all things are ordained for the use of humankind to bind us in obedience and obligation to God; 3) humankind is endowed with reason and thus distinguished from animals that they might meditate on and desire God in whose image they were made; 4) next comes the story of the fall of Adam which deprives him of all uprightness, alienates him from God, and leaves him perverse in heart and under the sentence of eternal death.

This all seems as would be expected. However, at this point, Calvin surprises us when he continues: 5) Moses then adds the "history of the restoration of humanity where Christ shines forth with the benefit of redemption." According to Calvin, Genesis relates the providence of God in preserving the Church, shows us true worship of God, teaches us of the salvation of humankind, and uses examples of the Patriarchs to exhort us to endure the cross. Of course, for Calvin as well as for his contemporary exegetes, whether Roman Catholic or Reformers of different stripes, the word of God to the Patriarchs was founded on Christ. Calvin therefore says that all the pious who ever have lived have been sustained by the same promise by which Adam was first raised from the fall. Here we can assume he refers to Genesis 3:15, the *protoevangelium*, which was considered to be the gospel-before-the-gospel. This verse contains the words of the curse to the serpent: "I will put enmity between you and the woman, and between your seed and her seed; he shall bruise your head, and you shall bruise his heel." Because Moses was ordained to be a teacher of the Israelites, says Calvin, God also intended, through Moses, to testify to all ages that there is only one true God whom we worship. These, according to Calvin, are the main topics of the book of Genesis.

But how does Calvin understand Genesis to speak of redemption, to tell of the history of the restoration of humanity, to speak even of the grace of Jesus, and to speak as clearly to sixteenth century Geneva as to Israel of antiquity? It is not merely the one verse of the *protoevangelium* which does this for Calvin. Rather, we see how the whole commentary turns on the assumption of the coherence or wholeness of the book of Genesis, and indeed the unity of the overall story of Israel, the people of God, the Church. However, this assumption has less to do with Calvin's understanding of the nature of the text itself than with the understanding of the nature of the God who addresses the faithful through the text. That is, the fact that the Bible is read as a continuous story is not on account of the nature of stories in general, nor the compelling nature of this story in particular, although to be sure Calvin does find this story compelling. The unitary and absorptive character of this particular biblical narrative issues from the prior claim of the unity and faithfulness of God.

We might illustrate this thesis by outlining two general categories or practices of reading which Calvin uses throughout the Genesis commentary to set forth the character of the One God whom Calvin trusts as both Author and subject matter of the biblical text. These two general categories can be seen to fall under the larger rubric of figurative reading.[10] The first is the reading of biblical stories as example. That is, Calvin holds up the lives of the Patriarchs as examples to his readers which illustrate the struggles of the Christian life. In this first category, the Patriarchs serve as "types" or figures which are reiterated daily in the life of the reader. The predicaments and perils, temptations and trials of the Patriarchs are gathered up and reappear in the life of the Christian, not merely incidentally but necessarily so, because the God with whom they all had to deal is the same God.

The first kind of figural reading is contingent upon a second kind, which entails a specifically Christological figurative hermeneutics. This second kind is reading biblical stories as christological prophecy, that is, engaging in figural reading such that Christ and the patterns of his life depicted in the New Testament are understood to be figured proleptically in the story of Israel. Here Calvin sees the story of Christ crucified and risen to be retrojected or folded in backwards· into the narratives of Israel. Like the egg-whites folded into a cake batter, it is this foretelling of the Christ-event in the stories of the Patriarchs which binds the canonical story together for Calvin. It enables and indeed requires him to read Genesis as the "Christian story". The "Argument" thus opens his commentary by setting the framework within which the figurative rendering of the Christian story takes place: Genesis is both an episode within and a proleptic vision of the Gospel story as a whole.

There are two sub-groups of the first type of figural reading. One is moral example, and the other is Christologically-rendered example. There are many instances of the first sub-group throughout Calvin's commentary on Genesis; the Patriarchs serve as examples of both positive and negative responses to the will and grace of God. Calvin used these examples to warn, console, and strengthen his audience in their daily struggles. Indeed, the Patriarchs can serve as positive examples of behavior which readers are to emulate, as we find in Calvin's comments on Genesis 22. Here, Abraham serves as an example of obedience and subjection to the will of God even in the thick of severe testing. There are, moreover, also instances of story as negative example, such as Abraham's palming off Sarah as his sister first on Pharaoh and then on Abimilech, and Sarah's impatience at the delay of the promise which prompts her to suggest that Hagar bear the son whom they await. In addition to citing stories as positive and negative examples, there are also instances in which Calvin rejects the possibility that a story could serve as example at all, as in his comments on the story of Abraham's servant offering Rebekah the gold jewelry in Genesis 24:22:

> But it may be asked whether God approves ornaments of this kind, which pertain not so much to neatness as to pomp? I answer that the things related in Scripture are not always proper to be imitated. Whatever the Lord commands in general terms is to be accounted as an inflexible rule of conduct; but to rely on particular examples is not only dangerous, but even foolish and absurd.[11]

The general use of the Patriarchs as examples is linked only indirectly with Calvin's broader, implicit understanding of the absorptive character of the biblical narrative. That is, these instances conceivably could have been part of his comments even if he did not understand the Christ-story to be typologically rendered in the Patriarchs' lives. Thus, this sub-group can be classified simply as moral application. While this in itself would be useful for building the character of Calvin's listeners, moral application is not what makes us companions of the Patriarchs, not what draws us into the "strange new world within the Bible". If it were this alone, we would also be the companions of the characters of any other moral narrative.

More interesting for our present purposes is the second sub-group, in which the Patriarchs and their struggles are portrayed as directly figurative of the lives of Christians who follow them. A straightforward instance of this is found in Calvin's comments on the story of Jacob wrestling at the Jabbok in Genesis 32. The purpose of this story, according to Calvin, is

> to represent all the servants of God in this world as wrestlers; because the Lord exercises them with various kinds of conflicts … Therefore, what was once exhibited under a visible form to our father Jacob, is daily fulfilled in the individual members of the Church; namely, that in their temptations it is necessary for them to wrestle with God …[12]

Jacob's struggle with the strange assailant at the Jabbok, according to Calvin, is a figure of the struggle of the Christian life which can be seen to be recapitulated in the struggles of Calvin's contemporary parishioners. In similar manner, when commenting on the murder of Abel in Genesis 4:10 at the phrase, "the voice of thy brother's blood crieth from the ground", Calvin says:

> This is a wonderfully sweet consolation to good men who are unjustly harassed, when they hear that their own sufferings, which they silently endure, go into the presence of God of their own accord to demand vengeance … Nor does this doctrine apply merely to the state of the present life, to teach us that among the innumerable dangers by which we are surrounded we shall be safe under the guardianship of God; but it elevates us by the hope of a better life, because we must conclude that those for whom God cares shall survive after death …[13]

Thus Abel's own silent death and the crying of his blood to God for vengeance is a lesson for Calvin's listeners (and, Calvin would say, to us in our turn) that they should submit in their suffering with the knowledge of and trust in God's care, for this is the pattern of the innocent suffering of the vindicated Risen Lord. Remarkably, Calvin in effect says that the story of Cain and Abel assures us of the doctrine of the resurrection of the dead. However, instead of stating this explicitly, he illustrates it by portraying the story of Abel's innocent suffering as a type for our own suffering, one which we recapitulate whenever we face suffering in the hope of God's vindication which we see in the resurrection of Christ.

Calvin uses the story of God's establishment of the covenant with Noah after the flood in Genesis 9 to argue against his theological rivals. At verse 9, which reads "with you and your seed after you", Calvin claims that:

> the ignorance of the Anabaptists may be refuted who deny that the covenant of God is common to infants, because they are destitute of present faith ...[14]

Two things in particular are to be noted here. First, the story has direct application to one of the theological debates which Calvin faces, namely, his disagreement with the Anabaptists over infant baptism. According to Calvin, the very words of the text ("with you and your seed after you") indicate a direct refutation of the Anabaptist position. Second, an obvious implication of this line of argumentation is that the covenant with Noah *is* the covenant of baptism, namely, the covenant sealed in the death and resurrection of Christ. Notice how different Calvin's argument is from a strictly "salvation-historical" plan in which God reveals himself in successively clearer covenants until the crowning glory of the covenant mediated by Christ. Here is an instance of our companionship with a "patriarch", Noah, based on the understanding that the Christ-story is proleptically present in Noah's story and analeptically present in ours. The absorptive capacity of the Biblical texts thus works multi-directionally: the Christ-story is absorbed into Noah's, Noah's into Christ's, and both into ours.

At the story of Abraham's offering of the animals and birds in Genesis 15, Calvin tries to avoid the "fabrication of subtleties" and the "wander(ing) in uncertain speculations." Instead, he wants to "cultivate sobriety", saying that the sum of this story is:

> That God, in commanding the animals to be killed, shows what will be the future condition of the Church. Abram certainly wished to be assured of the promised inheritance of the land. Now he is taught that it would take its commencement from death; that is that he and his children must die before they should enjoy the dominion over the land ... We see, therefore, that two things were illustrated; namely, the hard servitude, with which the sons of Abram were to be pressed almost to laceration and destruction; and then their redemption, which was to be the signal pledge of divine adoption; and in the same mirror the general condition of the Church is represented to us as it is the peculiar providence of God to create it out of nothing, and to raise it from death.[15]

Thus the "simple sense" of the offering narrated in Genesis 15 tells us of the future condition of the church, of Abram's descendants and the church of Calvin's day recapitulating the death and resurrection of the one who calls them into being in their suffering and their hope for the promise.[16] If we wondered how Calvin could see redemption "figuring" into the Genesis story as he claimed in his "Argument", here it is. The attaining of the promised land after the hardships of slavery and the wandering in the desert is a figure of Christ, and, because of this, it is also a figure of the Church which shares in the sufferings of Christ. This story of Abram's offering, which Calvin admits is obscure ("I shall not be ashamed to acknowledge my ignorance …," he states) figuratively represents the existence of the Church, and therefore serves as a word of hope. This chain of figures works because Calvin sees the offering story to hold within itself both the recollection of creation *ex nihilo*, narrated fourteen chapters earlier, and the promise of the redemption yet to be narrated in the New Covenant.

The second category, christological-prophetic typology, is less prevalent than either sub-group of the first category throughout Calvin's commentary on Genesis. However, its scarcity makes the typology all the more striking when it does appear, especially in view of Calvin's many comments disparaging allegorical "speculations". He generally holds allegorical reading in contempt for its "corruption" of Scripture's literal sense. For example, at Genesis 49:1 Calvin makes the following comment.

> Thus it has happened, that in striving earnestly to elicit profound allegories, they have departed from the genuine sense of the words and have corrupted, by their own inventions what is here delivered for the edification of the pious. But lest we should depreciate the literal sense, as if it did not contain speculations sufficiently profound, let us mark the design of the Holy Spirit …[17]

For Calvin, the text at face value, the "way the words go", is itself spiritually and theologically profound enough that one should not have to layer the text with allegorical embroidery.[18] Again, also at Genesis 49:12, he makes a similarly disparaging comment about overly imaginative readings of the biblical text:

> I abstain from those allegories which to some appear plausible; because, as I said at the beginning of the chapter, I do not choose to sport with such great mysteries of God …[19]

Despite these comments, occasionally Calvin will approve openly of a specific allegorical reading, such as in his discussion at Genesis 27:27:

> The allegory of Ambrose on this passage is not displeasing to me. Jacob, the younger brother, is blessed under the person of the elder; the garments which were borrowed from his brother breathe an odour grateful and pleasant to his father. In the same manner we are blessed, as Ambrose teaches, when, in the name of Christ, we enter the presence of our heavenly Father: we receive from him the robe of righteousness which, by its odour, procures his favour; in short, we are thus blessed when we are put in his place …"[20]

Just as it was Ambrose's figurative reading of the Old Testament which "redeemed" the Bible for Augustine and opened his heart to the catholic Christian faith, so it is such figurative reading which allows Calvin's observations recorded in his "Argument" to come to fruition in the commentary. His claim that "we are companions of the Patriarchs", based as it is on the Oneness of God, demands a reading of the Bible which embraces the canon as a whole, and sometimes requires allegorical or typological readings. For example, in expounding the story of Jacob's dream of the ladder reaching to heaven at Gen 28:12, Calvin says:

> It is Christ alone, therefore, who connects heaven and earth: he is the only mediator who reaches from heaven down to earth ... If then, we say that the ladder is a figure of Christ and exposition will not be forced ... That the ladder was a symbol of Christ is also confirmed by this consideration, that nothing was more suitable than that God should ratify his covenant of eternal salvation in his Son to his servant Jacob. And hence we feel unspeakable joy when we hear that Christ, who so far excels all creatures, is nevertheless joined with us ...[21]

Again, we see that the absorptive capacity of the biblical text is multi-directional: from Jacob to Christ, from Christ to Jacob, from both to us. The multi-directional flow is from the Christ-story outward, both backward and forward. In this way, each Christian whom Calvin addresses shares with Jacob in the joy of being joined with Christ. As Calvin says, we have "fraternal society" with Jacob and the Patriarchs, because we share a common Head whose "station is on earth." Reading the ladder as a figure of Christ establishes a link not only between Jacob and God but also between Jacob and all those baptized into Christ's death and resurrection.

Calvin also reads the story of Jacob's blessing of Ephraim and Manasseh in christological-typological fashion. While he regards as absurd the reading which interprets the crossing of Jacob's hands to signify the cross of Christ,[22] he does advocate reading the word "angel" at 48:16 christologically.

> Wherefore it is necessary that Christ should be here meant, who does not bear in vain the title of Angel, because he had become the perpetual Mediator. And Paul testifies that he was the Leader and Guide of the journey of his ancient people (1 Cor 10:4). He had not yet indeed been sent by the Father to approach more nearly to us by taking our flesh, but because he was always the bond of connection between God and man, and because God formally manifested himself in no other way than through him, he is properly called the Angel. To which may be added that the faith of the Fathers was always fixed on his future mission ...[23]

In reading the angel as Christ Calvin shows that he is assuming that Christ is, and always has been, the "bond of connection" between God and humanity. Therefore, he also assumes, without sensing that he is "adding" anything to the text or embroidering allegories, that the angel whom Jacob declares to have redeemed him *has to have been* Christ, whose office it is "to defend and to deliver us from all evil." Because of this, argues Calvin, it is indeed proper to say that the faith of the Fathers was fixed on the future mission of Christ, the same object of faith shared by Calvin's listeners. Christ is absorbed into the angel of the Genesis blessing, and the angel into Christ. It is this which renders Calvin's listeners as companions of the Patriarchs.

There are many such examples within Calvin's commentary on Genesis, as well as in his other commentaries and sermons. What then can we learn from these about the absorptive power of the biblical text for the narrative reader? First, Calvin's commitment to the unity of the biblical narrative does not arise from a belief that story is a theological category, or from an assumption that the category of narrative mirrors a universal psychological structure in the human soul. In both those examples of Calvin's interpretation in which the Christian struggle is figured in the lives of the Patriarchs, and in those in which Christ is figured in the stories about the Patriarchs, the significant element is this: Calvin does not *establish* a canonical unity via such figural interpretation, but rather such interpretation *assumes* an understanding of canonical unity, which is a corollary of the Church's affirmation of the unity of God's will and work.

Second, Calvin begins with the assumption of canonical unity because he holds a prior assumption of the unity of God. That is, the formal basis of canonical wholeness is the oneness of the divine reality and voice, the God who in Christ appears throughout the gospel stories, in the stories of Genesis, throughout the entire Bible, and indeed in the lives of Calvin's own parishioners and students. Third, this formal unity is exhibited occasionally via figural interpretation, and at times even demands it. Thus, the Bible is read as a single, cumulative narrative, but not as a direct result of any specific hermeneutical practice. Calvin cannot abandon figural reading entirely despite the stock Reformation polemic against allegory, not because of his understanding of what it means to read a text *qua* text, but because of his understanding of the God of Israel and of the nature of the biblical text. That is, Calvin's fugue of figural and literal reading is not an *apriori* commitment to a specific hermeneutical methodology in order to unify this random collection of narratives which he knows as the Old Testament. Rather, his interplay of literal and figural interpretation is an *ad hoc* practice used to interpret the Scriptures on which the Church's faith stands, the faith which trusts in God's divine care-taking over the storied history which the text is understood to depict.

Whatever we may learn from Calvin about reading the Bible, either positively or negatively, the task, of course, falls to us in our own day to listen for and to heed the voice of the Living God addressing us and our contemporaries. It does seem, in any case, that those theological claims which guide Calvin's reading of the Bible and allow it to absorb his world are bound up as a package in what it means to read the Bible as Scripture. Auerbach's statement about the Bible's overcoming our reality, after all, is based on a literary observation only because the literary text examined happens to be the Bible, and the Bible happens to make strong theological assumptions about what counts for "reality." Will we allow the Bible to absorb our world, in Auerbach's words, "to overcome our reality ... not merely to make us forget our own reality for a few hours?" If we do, there is a multiplicity of readings which can result, a deep well gushing ever forth. If not, we might want to be honest and admit that, instead of being companions of the patriarchs, we are merely "reading someone else's mail."[24]

NOTES

1 This article is adapted from a presentation to the Reformed Theology and History Consultation of the American Academy of Religion, November 1993.

2 The term "the Yale school" will be heuristically useful at this point, even though the Yale school itself is a many-faced phantom whose true existence many doubt. The same may be said for the "narrative theology" associated with the "Yale school". Those who are credited with being the leaders of the "Yale school" and its "narrative theology" have questioned the terms' applicability to themselves. For example, see Hans W. Frei, " 'Narrative' in the Christian and Modern Reading," in *Theology and Dialogue: Essays in Conversation With George Lindbeck*, ed. Bruce Marshall (Notre Dame, IN: University of Notre Dame Press, 1990), p. 161; Brevard S. Childs, *The New Testament as Canon: An Introduction* (Philadelphia, PA: Fortress Press, 1982), pp. 541–547; William C. Placher, *Domestication of Transcendence: How Modern Thinking About God Went Wrong* (Louisville, KY: Westminster/John Knox Press, 1996), p. xi.

3 George A. Lindbeck, *The Nature of Doctrine: Religion and Theology in a Post-Liberal Age*, (Philadelphia, PA: Westminster, 1984), p. 118.

4 Frei, in turn, is influenced by Erich Auerbach's observation in his book, *Mimesis: The Representation of Reality in Western Literature*, which Frei quotes shortly after the above: "Far from seeking, like Homer, merely to make us forget our own reality for a few hours, [the Old Testament narrative] seeks to overcome our reality: we are to fit our own life into its world, feel ourselves to be elements in its structure of universal history ... Everything else that happens in the world can only be conceived as an element in this sequence; into it everything that is known about the world ... must be fitted as an ingredient of the divine plan." Hans W. Frei, *The Eclipse of Biblical Narrative: A Study in Eighteenth and Nineteenth Century Hermeneutics* (New Haven, CT: Yale University Press, 1974), p. 3.

5 Bruce Marshall, "Absorbing the World: Christianity and the Universe of Truths," in *Theology and Dialogue*, p. 69.

6 Of course, it is no longer *au courant* among theologically educated Westerners to speak of God as the author of Scripture. For a sophisticated consideration of how we might reappropriate this notion, see Nicholas Wolterstorff, *Divine Discourse: Philosophical Reflections on the Claim That God Speaks* (Cambridge: Cambridge University Press, 1995).

7 Frei, *The Eclipse of Biblical Narrative* (New Haven, CT: Yale University Press, 1974), pp. 33, 36.

8 George Lindbeck, "Scripture, Consensus, and Community," in *Biblical Interpretation in Crisis*, ed. Richard John Neuhaus (Grand Rapids, MI: Wm. B. Eerdmans Publishing Co., 1989), p. 75.

9 John Calvin, *A Commentary on the Book of Genesis*, trans. John King (Grand Rapids, MI: Baker Book House, 1979), p. 66.

10 For the purposes of this essay I will use the terms "figural", "figurative", and "typological" interchangeably for all non-literal reading. I will use the term "allegory" to signify this same phenomenon in the context of discussion where Calvin himself chooses this term. Following James Barr ("Typology and Allegory", *Old and New in Interpretation*, New York, NY: Harper and Row, 1966), I am not assuming an airtight distinction between allegory and typology, and I do not think that Calvin held such a distinction either.

11   Calvin, op. cit., Vol. 2, pp. 22–23.

12   Ibid., pp. 195–196.

13   Ibid., Vol. 1, pp. 207–208.

14   Ibid., p. 298.

15   Calvin, op. cit., Vol. 2, pp. 413–414.

16   Calvin does not use the specific phrase "simple sense" here, but he does use it elsewhere in opposition to such phrases as "uncertain speculations", etc. It seems clear from the context that he does not claim to be adding anything to the text in offering this interpretation, and therefore we can assume that Calvin would not call this interpretation "uncertain speculation".

17   Calvin, op. cit., Vol. 2, p. 439.

18   The phrase "the way the words go" is from Bruce Marshall's translation and description of Thomas' biblical interpretation in Marshall, op. cit. While I would expand Marshall's description of how the "plain sense" is understood, his phrase is nevertheless useful for the present discussion. See my *Ad Litteram: How Augustine, Calvin and Barth Understood the 'Plain Sense' of Genesis 1–3*, forthcoming with Peter Lang.

19   Calvin, op. cit., Vol. 2, p. 451.

20   Ibid., p. 91.

21   Ibid., pp. 113–114.

22   Ibid., p. 432.

23   Ibid., pp. 428–429.

24   This itself is a huge topic. See, for example, the very different positions of Paul Van Buren, "On Reading Someone Else's Mail: The Church and Israel's Scriptures," in *Die Hebräische Bibel und Ihre Zweifache Nachgeschichte, FS R. Rendtorff* Erhard Blum, et al., eds., (Neukirchen-Vluyn: Neukirchener, 1990), pp. 595–606, and Christopher Seitz, "Old Testament or Hebrew Bible: Some Theological Considerations," *Pro Ecclesia* Vol. 5 No. 3 (Summer, 1996): pp. 292–303.

"IS THERE A (NON-SEXIST) BIBLE IN THIS CHURCH?" A FEMINIST CASE FOR THE PRIORITY OF INTERPRETIVE COMMUNITIES

MARY McCLINTOCK FULKERSON

My essay title is a play on a book title of a few years ago, *Is There a Text in This Class? The Authority of Interpretive Communities*. With this provocative question literary critic Stanley Fish means to disrupt the basic assumption of most hermeneutical theory, namely, that proper interpretation must work with an objective text or dissolve into subjectivism.[1] Fish's answer is a yes and a no. Of course there is a text, but to know what it is you must attend to the interpretive conventions on its subject as these are represented by the professor. There is not a text in the class, however, if "text" means an entity with fixed and enduring meaning. The meaning of a text is the creation of an interpretive community. Meaning is constrained by communal rules for reading, and not by some "objective" perspicuous sense contained within a text. Fish's query is an invitation to consider his alternative to the false hermeneutical dilemma of objective vs. subjective, namely, that texts are constructions of interpretive communities.[2]

I take that invitation to be useful for feminist theological thinking about biblical interpretation. Relocating attention from the bible itself to the site of interpretive communities and their conventions is a good move for thinking about a feminist dilemma, namely, whether there is a non-sexist bible in the church. Focus on interpretive communities will help avoid essentialist answers about the kind of text the bible is, particularly to such questions as whether it is harmful or liberating for women in an absolute way. Just as feminists have been exploring the differences among "women" over the past decade, we need a similar recognition of the *different* biblical texts that are

Mary McClintock Fulkerson
Duke Divinity School, Durham, NC 27708, USA

read by women differently positioned by racialized patriarchal capitalism.[3] In order to answer "what kind of bible?" we need to ask, "what kind of church/communities and conventions? what kind of women?" To begin this process I will first suggest how Fish's notion of communal conventions is helpful to feminist concerns. Following a brief consideration of the disturbance a shift to communities creates for traditional notions of the biblical text, I will end with a display of a further developed Fishian approach by looking at a community of women and the biblical "text" they construct.

Feminist[4] Hermeneutics: Why We Need Fish

Feminist and other liberation processes of theological reflection are notorious for eschewing formalism. These theologies get started with an interchange between contemporary situations of social critical consciousness—of crisis— and tradition. As Latin American liberationist Juan Segundo puts it, a new liberation hermeneutic emerges when the issues arising out of contemporary situations are serious enough "to force us to change our customary conceptions of life, death, knowledge, society, politics, and the world in general." There must be a change in "customary interpretation of the Scriptures," and the initation of the hermeneutical circle occurs with "profound and enriching questions about our real situation."[5] More radical with the biblical hermeneutics of suspicion than Latin American liberationists, feminists share the conviction that concerns arising out of empirical social situations generate a new theological and biblical hermeneutic.

Anti-formalism is good for a feminist approach because it assumes that context and use rather than language in its abstract (non-empirical) forms constitute the site of meaning. Such an approach to interpreting "women's" practices can better honor differences without ignoring the forces of racialized patriarchal capitalism.[6] Existent feminist and Womanist approaches already recognize this to a great degree. An important thread in all of feminist and Womanist thinking over the decades, notes Elizabeth Castelli, is "the assertion that reading and interpretive strategies are socially, politically, and institutionally situated, and that they draw their energy and force from the subject positions of readers and interpreters."[7] Womanist theology has long challenged the tendency in whitefeminism to judge the bible as hopelessly misogynist and goes a long way toward decentering interpretation. However, feminist thinking has not gone far enough in the deformalization process. Feminist habits of ascribing agency and power to the text continue to occlude the way in which the harm and beneficence of scripture is only intelligible through the conventions of a community. Fish's radical anti-formalism helps explore that in new ways.[8] Let me explain.

It may seem that the alternatives decried by Fish—objective vs. subjective meanings, the former necessary to avoid the anarchy of the latter—are straw targets, since avowed positivists in biblical studies are rare these days. The old academic charge that feminist interpreters were "subjectivists" is also dated. However, accepting the contextual character of interpretation is not the same as Fish's refusal of linguistic/textual formalism. The latter goes beyond the context-sensitive approach (of reader-response as well as liberation hermeneutics) to "disappear" the interpreter-text distinction into interpretive communities.[9]

This radical move is necessary to combat the enemy of textual formalism, the notion that meaning is a feature of abstract relations in language apart from use.[10] As Fish puts it, not only is the meaning of a sentence not "a function of the meaning of its constituent parts," but

> meaning cannot be formally calculated, derived from the shape of marks on a page; or to put it in the most direct way possible, that there is no such thing as literal meaning, if by literal meaning one means a meaning that is perspicuous no matter what the context and no matter what is in the speaker's or hearer's mind, a meaning that because it is prior to interpretation can serve as a constraint on interpretation.[11]

To break the habit of "literal meaning" Fish asks that we take a counter-intuitive posture toward what has been naturalized, that is, made to seem given or natural, as opposed to constructed. The assumption that the black marks on the page are writing, that the leather bound rectangular object is something to read rather than, say, sit on—all of these are conventions of communities. Rhetorical patterns found in the text, whether of the "echoes of scripture" found in Paul, as one NT scholar put it, or the "patriarchal stamp of scripture," as a feminist interpreter put it, are actually a function of one's interpretive grid. This does not mean that communities cannot construe an interpretive line in a text and claim that it serves as a constraint on interpretation (what is called the plain sense, a topic for later); however, this is still a convention, and it comes from corporate patterns and institutionally shaped interests of communities, not from the private psyche of an individual reader or supposed text-in-itself.[12]

The larger problem for feminist hermeneutics is that formalism can occlude agency behind ascription of responsibility to a text or to rules. Fish directs us to look at the way an interpretive community's conventions "make" the text and opens up the possibility of examining the ways that interest and desire are occluded by ascription of agency to texts. While we will inevitably use the rhetoric of texts and interpreters, failure to explore the conventions that constitute the text is problematic. For example, on Fish's terms to grant the biblical text responsibility for the church's homophobia is to "find" in the text all sorts of meanings which in fact require particular shared theological assumptions, acts of unifying and selection. Likewise, to ascribe misogyny or sexism to the bible, as we feminists often do, is also to deploy communal conventions that have to do with our place in and way of articulating the world. This acknowledgement does not render either view pointless or wrong (although I would only defend one). It *does* mean that accounts of what is in the text are extensions of deeply embedded interests, articulations of the world, and, going beyond Fish, I would say constraints that include relations of power.[13] The task of a feminist theologian, then, is to find the conventions, the institutional and larger socio-economic and political forces that support the interpretive grids of communities.

The Destabilized Text: In Need of a Theological Rescue?

Anti-formalism will aid feminist and other liberation hermeneutics in the interrogation of social location, but we also need locating in the Christian tradition, and for many, that means Christian scripture. How can we talk about the way various traditions of Christian faith do shape Christian communities, especially given that many speak of the "primacy of scripture"? Given the complexity of these issues, a realistic question for this essay is how the stability of the text might be rendered intelligible in anything like what Christian theology (especially Protestant) has assumed about the authority of scripture with this kind of move to interpretive communities. First, it must be clear that the typical fear Fish elicits, namely, that this anti-formalism is an invitation to fantasy and "mere" preference, is simply unnecessary. Communal convictions and the deeply embedded habits that constrain them guide interpretation, not private whim. Fish says, "there is no such thing as a 'mere preference' in the sense that makes it a threat to communal norms, for anything that could be experienced as a preference will derive from the norms inherent in some community." To paraphrase him, "all biblical interpretive preferences are shaped by theological interpretive grids (principles), e.g., they are intelligible only by virtue of a theological (principled) articulation of the world; and all theological interpretive grids (principles) are preferences, because every such grid (principle) is an extension of a particular view of the world that is *contestable* and as a perspective, it cannot be universal."[14] Given the inescapability of constraints, this means "stability" is relocated from what I judge to be the false security of fixed meaning to different, conflicting theological communal grids and the practices that embody them.

Given the turn to communal grids and practices, postliberal theology would seem useful for an anti-formalist theological proposal. This theological type calls for the communal control of texts and a look at practice as the site where true "expertise" in judgments of faith should be located.[15] The postmodern biblical criticism of Hans Frei as developed by George Lindbeck and others into postliberal theology has turned to community-relative notions of scripture, designed to refute the effects of modern criticism on the biblical text. Frei's concerns are widely shared, as evidenced in a burgeoning phenomenon found in Jewish as well as Christian biblical scholars, says Peter Ochs. This phenomenon is characterized by the presumption that believing communities are the normative site for interpreting scriptural texts.[16] A brief consideration of this communal hermeneutics will help clarify the theological stakes of Fish's anti-formalism.

As is well known, Hans Frei argued that modern critical attitudes had impoverished biblical studies and proposed instead to recover the literal or realist-like narrative meaning of the text, e.g., its central sense as a narrative of Jesus Christ.[17] Frei's recovery of the literal sense was expanded by George Lindbeck and other postliberal theologians to other semiotic procedures purported to confine Christian meaning to its internal logic.[18] To this end, postcritical interpreters commend *intratextuality* (the production of meaning that is internal to the signifying process of scripture) as a kind of rule ensuring that the "biblical world" will have primary force in the shaping of communities, rather than "external" signifying processes (*extra*textuality). Extratextual approaches, such as treatments of the text as historical document and as container of symbols translatable into general existential truths, mistakenly regard the text as needing to be rendered universally intelligible. They destroy, or at least undermine, sometimes severely, the internal logic of the Christian faith.

The notion of intratextuality does not fully account for the "interpretive community" of postliberal theology. Lindbeck expands intratextuality (a primarily textual logic) to a cultural-linguistic model of the community (a logic of practice). Thus proper reading of the textual logic is constrained with a concept of a doctrinal grammar. Doctrines are not objective propositions, but rules that order Christian life and interpretation. Doctrines are grammatical rules about how properly to tell the story, an identity-forming narrative of Jesus Christ. A "thick description" of a faith community requires more than right speaking, however. Lindbeck's (Geertzian) culture theory helps articulate the conviction that habits, dispositions, actions, performance are the ways in which intratextual faithfulness is manifested. Thus it is a community that *practices* the story as well as *tells* it that can properly interpret the Bible.

Let me summarize and assess. When we pay attention to the interpretive community that has named and produced the conventions that so attribute and construe the text, we would say that it is *as used in a particular way* that the biblical text comes to have the meaning of this Jesus narrative and the supporting lexicon for living grammatically. Nothing illustrates this better than Lindbeck's insistence that practitioners are the best judges of faithful grammar. This considerable move away from the formalism of a text locates truthfulness in performance rather in the formal properties of a text. Such anti-formalism is designed to refute the notion of religiousness in general, offering instead a "normative explication of the meaning a religion has for its adherents" or the "informal logic of actual life." In one sense, then, grammar is a certain kind of communal *use* of a text.[19]

However, there is formalism at another level in this proposal and a second, overarching sense in which grammar is not used. Canonical texts are "a condition, not only for the survival of a religion, but for the very possibility of normative theological description," says Lindbeck. The source of the rules is mainly scripture. Indirectly, however, the rules come from theologians. The effect of empirical and historical change is duly noted—theological conceptualities change over time, theologians work to find the conceptuality best suited to 'say the same thing' in different terms. Again, they "say the same thing"; "the same content can be expressed in different formulations." Even as there is "variable theological vocabulary", there is "abiding doctrinal grammar."[20] The direction of semiosis is one-way: from the scriptural world "outward"; employing the rules one appropriates the "external" realities to the logic of the narrative. This communal hermeneutic brings with it a grammar that, even though it transcends the text and is defensible as a convention of use for scripture, is *fixed*. It is a system of rules produced by agents (theologians) who remain unavailable for interrogation.

The problem is not the construal of scripture as a narrative of Jesus Christ. Every community that uses scripture will have to create order out of it—construe it, in the words of David Kelsey. A Jesus story might well work as a critical sense that is used to assess other convictions.[21] The problem is the proposal that there is a fixed grammar controlling the story into which all difference could be rendered commensurable. Despite the intent to *combat* religious formalism by filling it with Christian content, imposition of such a grammar is another formalism. This is because it is posed as a system that can be discerned to be the same apart from occasions of use. The grammar is *abstract* ("without empirical content"); it is *general* ("not to be identified with any race, location or historical period but with the species"); and *invariant* ("does not differ from language to language," or social context, I would add).[22] Even as postliberal theology claims to resist the formalism of extratextuality and religiousness in general, it puts forward its own formal version of Christianity. Thus it cannot allow assessment of the ideological and occluded discourses in Christian communal life and sedimented traditions, which is necessary to a feminist theological interpretation of scripture.

I take from this communal hermeneutics two insights. First, attention to performance or use of scripture in particular contexts is a crucial move against formalism. If a faith is not embodied, it does not exist, no matter how protected and revered its scripture. In arguing that Christians use the locution of *performing* the scriptures, Nicholas Lash says that despite our talk of "holy scriptures", "it is not, in fact, the *script* that is 'holy', but the people: the company who perform the script."[23] It is a notion with which postcritical theologians seem utterly sympathetic: "(m)eaning is constituted by the uses of a specific language rather than being distinguishable from it ... (and) the proper way to determine what 'God' signifies, for example, is by examining how the word operates in a religion and thereby shapes reality and experience ... However, we cannot in fact determine what "God" signifies in a faith outside of real practices or performances of Christians.[24] Further, as

Kathryn Tanner insists, these practices will always be subject to dispute in a setting of dialogue and argument, not grounded or authorized by one commensurable grammar.[25]

In view of the requirement that theological analysis emerges from real practices, a second insight follows. Formalism cannot be removed by the theologian from one place only to be reintroduced at another (grammar or "literal sense"). Communal conventions will operate to construe scripture in Christian communities in some way, but the theologian cannot insist that the construal be controlled by a fixed system of meaning, which is "meaning that is perspicuous no matter what the context and no matter what is in the speaker's or hearer's mind, a meaning that because it is prior to interpretation can serve as a constraint on interpretation."[26] It is universal discourse; it is formalism, and it is what postliberal theology was created to correct.

To develop a non-formalist account of Christian faith which is historically embedded in practices of scripture, Kathryn Tanner's version of the plain sense of scripture makes more sense—"the obvious or direct sense of the text for the Christian community—what is established by communal consensus". The "plain sense" can be what a community understands to be the obvious sense: people can articulate that as the sense God intended, or the original intent of the author, but it can and must be describable by the theologian as "what is established by communal consensus." It is a communal convention; it can serve a critical function over against the other discourses of faith; it is not, however, the same for all communities.[27] This point holds for grammar as well. If theological work attends to real practices, it cannot predetermine what must happen on the basis of an abstract, formal grammar; grammars may and do change.

What is more, there is no reason to fear the anarchy and chaos attributed to giving up formal rules, as Fish said, because the alternative is not "private preferences" or subjectivism. It is doing what appears right in the context with the conventions of the community. From a real anti-formalist view that takes use seriously and the meaning a faith has for (good) practitioners seriously, there will be no one grammar. There will always be different accounts of the "rules" as well as the reading. Thus, we will expect that grammatical practice will look like enough appropriate wisdom drawn from the community in order to "get on with things."

One final observation before turning to a feminist account of a community of biblical practice. Fish claims there are no consequences to his account of texts. That is because there are no theories in the sense of abstract formal discourses that are a priori to practices. To assume that theory as abstract discourse *determines* practices is precisely what he is arguing against. His account, then, is not a "theory"; it is part of a practice. One result of this is that we do continue to interpret even if we agree that there is no formally existent text with a "real meaning" to be discovered. We continue to use "the metaphorics of critical language", as Stephen Moore puts it; we talk of interpreters and texts as if texts "do things."[28] We also continue to sponsor one reading over another, as I do in advocating a feminist perspective in this essay. This is not a contradiction; the Fishian view is itself embedded in communal conventions and convictions. Our beliefs stay in place. This anti-formalist account of scripture removes nothing. We are not released from believing something is the case, that one form of Christian life is better than another. We are only released from certain accounts of why our inter-pretation is the truth, namely, its correspondence to a realm of theological rationality unconnected to situations and their partiality. All that the anti-foundationalism of this position offers us "is an alternative account of how the certainties that will still grip us when we are persuaded to it came to be in place."[29]

Nor does this view, as Fish insists, contradict itself by positing its communal-relative account of interpretation as an absolute theoretical truth (apart from use). That would miss entirely the stakes of the claims made here. Since this account of texts is not a theory that claims epistemological status prior to its practice as a partial taking on things, it is as vulnerable to challenges as all accounts are.[30] It assumes something about the status of claims. Appropriated into a *theological* practice of interpretation, as I am doing here, it is defensible theologically as fitting with a non-idolatrous posture toward worldly entities such as knowledge. The kind of power that is assumed available to legitimate such claims, then, is the power of persuasion. That is, claims are enforced *rhetorically*.[31] To go down this anti-formalist path as a Christian feminist theo-logian is not to surrender convictions, impassioned witness and action. It is to forego the notion that by conforming to a system of theological conceptuality some added force accrues to a proposal. It is, in a sense, to rely upon persua-sion, testimony (in the case of theological claims), and the better argument. It is also to make sure that we as feminists look at all the operations of dis-course, rhetorical strategies and the hidden power constraints that support claims.

From this foray into a theological communal hermeneutics, some conclus-ions can be drawn for the next stage of my analysis, a look at the interpretive community of Presbyterian Women. The first is the most general. A non-formalist theological communal hermeneutic must respect the specificity of a particular biblical-doctrinal tradition—the conventions in which these women are embedded—and find a way to do this that does not depend upon a priori judgment of how the text can be used if the source of it be Christian or feminist. I have transferred the agency of the text from some correct account of its internal or intratextual meaning to the practices of the communities that read and construct it. I thereby hope to show how what is a "sexist text" that obliterates women's well-being for one community of women may not be that for another. Thus, I will illustrate two possibilities that extend feminist theological thinking on scripture. First, we can appre-ciate from a feminist perspective that women have constraints that work to limit their options, but, second, that they may be able to maneuver the constraints to make good news in creative ways that do not fit all situations. There *is* a bible in the church, so to speak, that supports the well-being of these women.

Three observations will have to suffice on the terms of assessing this view of scripture, given space limitations. First, the importance of bypassing the ostensible agency of the text to account for what ought or ought not be done, is the opportunity to treat the practices, institutions and social forces that constrain women as necessary to a sympathetic reading of their use of the bible. Second, to assess the biblical and canonical tradition as contributors, two markers are pertinent to Protestant interpretive communities. The notion of the "plain sense" of scripture can aid in interpreting a community's use of its biblical tradition as a source of self-criticism. Defined with some community-relativity, it allows a more nuanced reading of women's resistance. And as long as they are not claimed to be a priori to interpretation, communal conventions may be identified as grammatical constraints. I ask how the Presbyterian Women's practice of scripture is shaped by some piece of historic grammar and thereby valued as practice toward a good and Godly end. Third, the risk of this Fishian approach is unavoidable: to insist that it is *as used* to some good end that scripture has any worth is to acknowledge the power of the text without fixing its meaning prior to practice. This is to say that the medium of authority—what is compelling—in the Christian faith is related to performance and social location and that the kind of "stability" that attends practice is the best and most we can hope for. Faithful practice testifies to the truth of a faith, and, indirectly, of its scripture.[32]

Presbyterian Women Practice Scripture

With these theological emendations to my proposal for a community-based feminist account of scripture, I now turn to an historic group of women who are not feminists, but whose practices are instructive about how differently located women can use scripture to resist. Presbyterian Women (hereafter, PW) is a churchwomen's organization, first formed as turn-of-the-century mission groups, and that had its real heyday from then till the 1960s and early 1970s.[33] The end against which I interpret and assess the practices of PW is not conformity to a text or grammar, but a response of good news to the crisis identified by feminist and related theologies, namely, how can this particular construction of a subject "woman" (white middle class) be transformed by the practices of a Christian community committed to a vision of God's creatures as *imago Dei*?

The practices of these middle-class white subjects would, of course, be missed if we assumed that the biblical world defines and absorbs all other worlds, or that the patterns of male symbols and prohibitions on women in the bible have such misogynist force that they rendered these women non-agents. The bible is not the agent here, however, and to see what is, we also need to complicate the notion of interpretive community. There will be no monolithic and homogeneous Christian community subject to control by a whole system or properly ordered scripture. "Communities" are fractured. They are part of a social formation (intersecting economic, political and cultural processes) laden with hidden histories and occluded voices—a social landscape riven with power asymmetries. In what follows, I trace the conventions that go into the construction of a biblical text for Presbyterian Women by looking first at the systems of meaning and power in which they are embedded and which they share with other Christians and Presbyterians. That I will designate a "canonical system". Next I will identify an alternative regime of reading of their own, which I will define as a "register", a form of biblical practice with resistance as well as conformity to the canonical system.

The most powerful set of constraints on PW's scriptural practice is the *canonical system* that produces them—all that goes into making them practitioners of scripture. Thus, the phrase does not refer to the biblical canon, although it encompasses it, but to the differential relations that bring the biblical text into being and make it accessible for a particular community.[34] This system consists of explicit rules about reading—stated and operative hermeneutical ideas. It includes an account of the end of interpretation and faithful living as well: what kind of reader-practitioner does the community wish to produce? The reach of a canonical system is broader than the official tenets of a tradition; it also includes the hidden conditions for the reproduction of communal life and its mechanisms for distributing power. The conditions for reproducing a male-dominated or a class-based community, for restricting the official practice of preaching, for interpreting the Word, for example, are as essential to a canonical system as an official hermeneutics.

The scriptural practices of PW are forged in relation to the Reformed canonical system, generated by the 16th century Geneva community of John Calvin and developed later in Scottish and New World Presbyterianism. For Reformed Presbyterians the explicit and lasting ends of the community include justification by faith, glorifying God, living a disciplined life, and obeying scripture as primary authority. A special relationship obtains between the goal of making scripture primary and these other ecclesial ends, such that the explicit end of the canonical system is the faithful performance of scripture—a performance that should transform society as it does the believer. By mid-20th century, explicit traditional rules for reading scripture in this system include: a) interpret the unclear by the clear, b) the rule of love, c) the centrality of Christ as Word over words, and d) application of historical criticism.

For centuries an implicit rule in the canonical system also ordered access to authority, determining *who* can interpret and *who* can speak. With this point we acknowledge the embeddedness of so-called strictly theological discourse with the conventions of the larger social formation. From the turn of the 19th century to the 1960s in the U.S., the rules for reading in this community were explicitly gendered. Access to the official registers of authority was denied women on the basis of an ahistorical view of the biblical text, a rule attributed to scriptural prohibitions, until 1954 in the northern UPC (USA), and 1964 in the southern church (P.C.U.S.).[35] The ostensibly biblical views that supported women's confinement to the domestic sphere and exclusion from public discourse were also duplicated by cultural class discourses of complementary genders which permeated U.S. life well beyond the first half of the 20th century. These ideas that (white) women were nurturing, emotional, and 'private' in ideal relation to rational, distanced, and 'public' (white) men were part of reproducing the gendered domestic and public spheres of the social formation for years.

The constraints related to power are as important to the overt conventions of the religious communities and their rules of Christian practice in the make-up of interpretive communities. The canonical system includes the conditions for reproduction of a community, such as procedures for authorizing and legitimating its interpreters—for gatekeeping. In addition to the collaboration between Presbyterian views on gender claimed to be found in the scriptures and the similar complementary gender constructions of the surrounding culture, another aspect of the system is the *class location* of the community. Positioned in the middle and upper-middle class, the Presbyterian church has long been populated by large numbers of professionals. Part of the reproductive character of the canonical system are educational institutions (universities, seminaries), a middle class preoccupation in the 19th century, which produce authorities for the interpretive community—those who qualify for church leadership, both in parish and bureaucratic positions.

The effects of this system are significant for women because for some years these institutions produced gender-exclusive *accounts* of authority as well as male leaders. This aspect of the canonical system is less obvious in the concept of rules for reading, but is equally necessary in the reproduction of a community. For the power to define and disseminate what qualify as legitimate questions and criticism is paramount to controlling the gender (and race or class) exclusivity of an institution. In the case of the Presbyterian Church, educational institutions were strong and well-supported (as compared to a socially marginal group like Pentecostals). These institutions had a crucial part in controlling the dispersion of an important critical tool that eventually helped loosen the grip of male authority in the church. That tool was historical criticism applied to the bible, an approach that was only significantly disseminated after the 1940s.

Women practitioners suffer the imprint of their social location beyond their religious tradition. For 20th century Presbyterian Women that is the impact of racialized patriarchal capitalism on their well-being. The impact of this social formation creates different forms of oppression for differently positioned women. Processes that are marginalizing around gender alone are not equal to processes which produce poverty and its marginalization as well. The combination that exists for poor African–American women, when race penalties are added, may result in survival issues overriding the sense of gender oppression. The dependence of middle-class housewives, as most Presbyterian Women were, is an odd combination of vulnerability and privilege. On the one hand, they are unskilled and have been increasingly de-skilled by the takeover of domestic functions initiated with industrial capitalism. Often married to professionals, on the other, they are less likely to worry about survival issues and do not understand themselves to have race (whiteness). It is, in short, economic dependence that includes privilege.[36]

Having barely sketched the forces that construct subject positions for Presbyterian Women, let me illustrate how their practice of scripture can be understood in feminist theological terms. Whether by a standard feminist grid or a view of accurate interpretation of scripture these women do not "resist", in the first case, and they must be judged woeful amateurs in the second. Their years of silence on ordination and failure to take up feminist discourse suggest they were passive, oppressed and victimized by patriarchy. None of the ideas of feminist resistance appear; taken alone their exegetical comments look totally unoriginal. Thus, to grant their practices some status as an interpretive community is not to uncover a hidden revolution or intellectual pool. However, if we forego a notion of the real meaning of the text and read their practices intertextually with both the canonical system and their social location in view, another picture emerges. With a look at the particular register of their Christian life, a more interesting account of the "informal logic" of real Christian practice so dear to postliberals emerges.

Thus far I have laid out the larger interpretive constraints that are fundamental to what PW will do with scripture, i.e., their reading regime. Now I need to relate their distinctive practice with the canonical system, suggesting how they construct one kind of scripture rather than another. A useful category for this task is the socio-linguistic concept of *register*.[37] Register refers to typological communication, a situation of utterance around which social expectations have collected. Used by socio-linguists and literary theorists to differentiate types of language use, identification of a register helps get at the fact that *what* is said and *how* it is said are inseparable in communication. Three variables create a register and contribute to its distinctiveness: the field variable (content, ideas), the variable of tenor (form of address, the relation set up between speaker and audience) and the mode (the medium—written, oral, etc.). (An idea, for example, is altered by the mode of its delivery.) Some variables are tied to a social situation (as liturgy is to a religious service), and some are not (political argument). Register can be as broad as a technical language (legal discourse), or as narrow as prayer. What all have in common is conventional expectations—familiarity in a community. When conventional expectations are met, we recognize the register—a military command, for example. When they are transgressed in some way, a register can function to express resistance—such as the parodying of registers of respect by marginalized groups. By interpreting Presbyterian Women's discourse as a register, we can relate it to the canonical system in terms of both its fulfillment of expectations and its transgression of the same.

Given the limits of this essay, only a partial analysis of the discourse is possible, and I will draw mostly on what is *said*, the field variable. A fuller account would pay more attention to the how of the discourse and its subregisters. As an organization, PW has developed regular patterns of utterance —a monthly literature and programmatic materials and use. The setting of the discourse is group meetings (circles) where PW projects are organized. Briefly summarized, the *mode* of their discourse is periodical literature used in face-to-face communities of care and project management. As a monthly magazine of self-improvement, this literature communicates through pictures of mission as effectively as through its serious essay and short information and project-idea columns. (You cannot get the full communicative effect of PW without the visual.) The *tenor*, or mode of address, of PW discourse is primarily interpersonal, with tones of informality, chattiness, and friendliness. Its relational effect is egalitarian as it addresses the reader through moral invocation as an equal, competent hearer. That address is often in the form of moral inspiration, from a call to competence to an interrogatory moral inventory. The *field*, or ideas, take traditional Presbyterian themes (the God-centered life, etc.) and center them around themes of domesticity, self-improvement and mission to the world neighbor in need.

Their practice is clearly embedded in tradition. PW reproduce the grammar of their Reformed canonical system with its rules for reading, for the primacy of scripture and for who can interpret or speak publically, while avoiding the official register of authority, which prohibits women from preaching or speaking in 'promiscuous assemblies'. As Fish would say, they "find" in scripture what their complementarily gendered social world leads them to find. Along that line, they reproduce the civility of their class in their refusal to "misbehave", and their efforts constantly to reassure the men that they are not trying to create a separate church. However, they do go about creating their own vocation as homemakers for whom the world is the ultimate horizon of responsibility. Their literature and projects are galvanized around the themes of their God-given vocation as homemaker and caretaker for family, children, church, and society. The importance of the egalitarian tenor, when it dominates the discourse of moral imperative, is that it nuances the address to the PW reader as one who *can* achieve great things and who must become what she *is*, competent and important.

Here domestic discourse resonates with the romantic feminism of the capitalist culture of the period, which privatized the home and left housewives with the new job of managing consumption. However, PW's discourse ultimately stretches and breaks out of the discourse of privatization and consumerism that shaped women in the 1940s and 1950s, widening their calling by interpellating women as responsible not only for the home, but for the church, community and world as damaged by war, poverty, racism, alcoholism, and communism. PW saw that the vocation of the homemaker Christian who would glorify God was "to make a difference in the world" and that difference meant caring for the needy wherever s/he was.

Viewed as a whole, PW practice is a literature with programmatic practices. I designate their practice a register, a recognizable form of communication, because of the way their ideas, mode of communication and form of address interact to produce a distinctive communicative project. That project is the production of these women as competent agents who enact God's care for a domestic sphere without boundaries. They carve out a place for work, career, international relations and travel; they speak, teach each other, and become authorities. PW practice a discourse of self-production and world-transformation.

The effects of this register are not monolithically positive. Presbyterian Women's discourse is often disciplinary in a Foucaultian sense—both in field and tenor, as their literature commends the women to greater and greater responsibilities for the transformation of home, church, community and world in a social order where their position is fundamentally contradictory. The capitalism of the 20th century is such that individuals make no impact on politics. In this complex social order, women's literature subjects them to increasingly scrupulous forms of self-examination, including worry about motive, intent and success. In addition, the magazine format of the discourse contains sub-registers, which sometimes produce visually submissive postures for the women. Pictures of male "talking heads" or experts frequently accompany the didactic pieces, underwriting the traditional feminine passive receiver. However, even this format also allows for contradictions, for the women can read themselves into increasing numbers of pictures of women experts and stories of authoritative competent women actors in the late 1960s and 1970s. There is, then, an instability to this discourse; it can reproduce submissive femininity by demanding what cannot be done in a capitalist economy, and/or it can produce competence and activism.

I have described practice in a most material sense, yet I am proposing that this literature and its use in circles is ordered as a *"scriptural practice"* or reading regime in an intertextual (between the "texts" of canonical system and their regime), not an intratextual sense. This is because the women's practices are only intelligible within the discourses and rules of the Reformed/ Presbyterian canonical system which view these activities as the ends of a scripture-based life. The bible is studied in their literature, but the grid for that is narration of a God and savior who model ministry to the needy. Its dominant and most distinctive use is inscriptions of biblical passages about helping the needy on pictures of refugee children, poor Appalachians, faces of the hungry, and photo displays of the oppressed in every corner of the globe. The women have literally created a biblical text for which these portrayals are the canon within a canon. The bible is translated into a picture book of human need, and the gospel of Jesus is the invitation to address it. This is obvious biblical practice, but I am saying more: that it is not intelligible without the foregoing account of the canonical system—the set of communal and institutional and larger social constraints for its existence and reproduction.

My enlarged notion of interpretive community helps make particular feminist sense out of the practices of these women. The centrality of the field variable of global domesticity helps interpret their failure to take up gender criticism—they achieve a "public" in a way that does not require the risks entailed if an unskilled, economically dependent population were to choose the route of confrontation. Their acquiescence to what many of us identify as the sexist language of scripture, such as the employment of such terms as "God the Father," when read intertextually, could also be read to resonate with the family imagery that dominates their discourse. In other words, that language activates meanings about the world neighbor and evokes the women's accountability to the need of the neighbor, as much as it does the male nature of those who control her (and it certainly does that). We find a multi-valence in these symbols when we exegete the generating interpretive community.

I see their resistance as a productive employment of the themes in the Reformed tradition about world transformation as the purpose of the church. In a community with gendered and exclusivist rules for reading, these women created a register for their own speaking and interpretation of scripture. Clearly their register does not transgress social expectations in a direct way. The rules for gender complementarity are never challenged. Their practices reproduce heterosexuality; they rarely raise gender as an issue. However, their practices do push against the oppressions of their location—from both church and from capitalism's devaluing of the home. They take their "place", domesticity, but stretch it beyond the bounds that make it safe for a capitalist and patriarchal world. They create a register of authoritative competence for women and thereby refuse the limits of the gendered reading regime of the first half of 20th century American Presbyterianism. It is in this sense that a resisting or contesting register is emergent.

Conclusion: Used to a Good End?

It is difficult to assess this register as a biblical practice and to assess whether my case for the priority of interpretive communities is made. However, that is partly because any real example partakes of those features that I have earlier said necessarily characterize the authority of a community that attends most seriously to faithful practices. The bible PW produce is not objective, although their beliefs are held as truthful convictions. Their bible is only partial and addresses a particular context—the need to do something about (some) "women" in a Christian community that reluctantly gives them public space. PW's interpretive conventions certainly illustrate Fish's point that these grids do not get created out of subjective whim—they drew on and were limited by the conventions of reading available to them. If there is a "plain sense of scripture" in their interpretive community, it would be a story of Jesus as the model of their mission to the needy. This "Jesus" is a Jesus of the tradition—missing some pieces, as accounts always do—but given its twist by their calling and their limitations. It can be criticized but should be celebrated as well, because it gets forged out of conventions that allow them to refuse at least some of the pernicious constraints of their social location.

In PW's production of scripture, there were departures from received patterns. While I have not suggested any big departures from traditional grammar (or doctrine) such as feminist theology proposes, I have illustrated the way that processes of meaning are always altering the received tradition. No normative grammar can escape this, nor should it claim to. What is emerging in this fragmentary, slightly contesting biblical practice is the new view that women are fully *imago Dei*. It is partial, but a relevant piece of the grammar that enables us to continue in a setting where the primary pain is the denial of that truth. I judge this partial testimony to be persuasive mostly because it has been generated by good practitioners, good because they practiced scripture to a good end, the *extension* of the Reformed view of who can faithfully transform self and world as an honoring of God.[38]

As for feminist conclusions, I have tried to dissuade readers from the view that the biblical texts are *just* sexist or not. In fact, the texts are lots of things, and arguments over what scripture really means are less useful than attention to the communal conventions that constrain that judgment. In order to have, to name, to honor, a bible in the church we have to honor the community constructing it and thereby learn something about how and how not to live.

NOTES

1   Stanley Fish pursues these issues in an essay and book of the same name. See 'Is There a Text in This Class?' in *Is There a Text in This Class? The Authority of Interpretive Communities* (Cambridge, MA: Harvard University Press, 1980), pp. 303–321.

2   This does not mean there is no reality external to our minds. It is compatible with most non-naive realisms.

3   The intersecting forces of U.S. patriarchy, capitalism, and racism. The first is a social arrangement where maleness is hierarchically related to femaleness, the second locates subjects in relation to class, and the third refers to a form of racialization where being designated "of color" (in the U.S. case, "black") locates subjects at the "bottom" of power hierarchies. The phrase is a formal one, because the intersection of these forces is complex and differentiated relative to communities, and to subjects designated "women". All three constrain all U.S. communities. Thus racialization may not appear to be relevant to all-white groups of women, but the fact that they are constructed by culture to think they have no race indicates its power and presence.

4   Feminist, with a few exceptions, typically refers to views of white women. I indicate that by referring to Womanist and Mujerista as different strategies in which gender matters. Occasionally I will use the coinage "whitefeminism," which was coined by feminist Ellen Armour.

5   Juan Luis Segundo, S.J., *The Liberation of Theology* (Maryknoll, NY: Orbis Books, 1976), pp. 8–9.

6   The scare quotes acknowledge that "woman" is not a natural category. The important work of poststructuralism is a reminder that the gendered subject is a construction, thus I will treat a group, Presbyterian Women, who are historically identified as gendered female.

7   Elizabeth Castelli, 'Feminist and Womanist Criticism,' in George Aichele, et al. (eds.), *The Postmodern Bible: The Bible and Culture Collective* (New Haven, CT: Yale University Press, 1995), p. 267.

8   Fish has not been used by feminist or other liberationist biblical interpreters, as far as I know, probably because he does not tackle ideology and social formation issues. Stephen D. Moore presses the implications of Fish's work for biblical criticism in a most interesting way. See 'Negative Hermeneutics, Insubstantial Texts: Stanley Fish and the Biblical Interpreter,' *Journal of the American Academy of Religion* Vol. 54 No. 4 (Winter, 1986), pp. 707–719.

9   See Stephen Moore's comments on this in his 'Negative Hermeneutics,' pp. 712–714.

10 I am using an abbreviated definition of formalism, focusing on the principles that meanings are a property of language, and that language is an abstract system prior to occasions of use. Fish directs readers to Roberto Unger for a longer discussion. See Fish, 'Introduction: The Anti-Formalist Road,' in *Doing What Comes Naturally: Change, Rhetoric, and the Practice of Theory in Literary and Legal Studies* (Durham, NC: Duke University Press, 1989), pp. 6–8.

11 Ibid., p. 4.

12 This theory about texts has no consequences; that is, one does not stop making interpretive judgments, one merely has a new take on where they come from. This argument is made by Fish in a number of places. For a straightforward treatment see his 'Consequences,' *Critical Inquiry* Vol. 11 No. 3 (March, 1985), pp. 433–458.

13 Fish's later work acknowledges this criticism. But see *The Postmodern Bible*, pp. 55–59.

14 Fish, 'The Anti-Formalist Road,' p. 11.

15 I refer to Lindbeck's definition of "intelligibility as skill" in his book on doctrine. I think he has two contradictory impulses in his account; one is his use of practice and the other a kind of linguistic structuralism he borrows from Ferdinand de Saussure. See George Lindbeck, *The Nature of Doctrine: Religion and Theology in a Postliberal Age* (Philadelphia, PA: Westminster Press, 1984), p. 128.

16 Peter Ochs, 'Introduction to Postcritical Scriptural Interpretation,' in Peter Ochs (ed.), *The Return to Scripture in Judaism and Christianity: Essays in Postcritical Scriptural Interpretation* (New York, NY: Paulist Press, 1993), pp. 3–51.

17 This is most forcefully articulated in Hans W. Frei, *The Eclipse of Biblical Narrative: A Study in Eighteenth and Nineteenth Century Hermeneutics* (New Haven, CT: Yale University Press, 1974).

18 John E. Thiel discusses this in his *Nonfoundationalism* (Minneapolis, MN: Fortress Press, 1994), pp. 38–78.

19 Lindbeck, pp. 113, 115.

20 Ibid., pp. 118, 113.

21 David H. Kelsey, *The Uses of Scripture in Recent Theology* (Philadelphia, PA: Fortress Press, 1975).

22 Stanley Fish, 'Consequences,' pp. 435–436.

23 While Lash's position is not the same as Fish's, its similarity in contrast with the postliberal view is that the constraints for Lash are historical intentions, "what it originally meant". This, as Fish points out, is an interpretive phenomenon, and subject to debate, not a formalist one. Nicholas Lash, 'Performing the Scriptures' in *Theology on the Way to Emmaus* (London: SCM Press Ltd., 1986), pp. 37–94. Fish, 'Anti-Formalist Road,' pp. 7–8.

24 Hans Frei quotes Lindbeck approvingly here in 'The "Literal Reading" of Biblical Narrative in the Christian Tradition: Does it Stretch or Will it Break?' abridged and edited by Kathryn Tanner in Ochs (ed.), *Return to Scripture*, p. 77.

25 Kathryn Tanner, *Theories of Culture: A New Agenda for Theology* (Minneapolis, MN: Fortress Press, 1997).

26 Fish, 'Anti-Formalist Road,' p. 4.

27   Kathryn E. Tanner, 'Theology and the Plain Sense,' in Garrett Green (ed.), *Scriptural Authority and Narrative Interpretation*, (Philadelphia, PA: Fortress Press, 1987), pp. 76 (n.14), 65–67, 59–78. She departs from Frei and Lindbeck, who maintain the grammar along with the (unproblematic) narrative plain sense most clearly in her book.

28   Moore, 'Negative Hermeneutics,' p. 709.

29   Fish, 'Anti-Formalist Road,' p. 26.

30   Ibid., pp. 29–30.

31   Fish, 'Rhetoric,' in *Doing What Comes Naturally*, pp. 471–502. Fulkerson, *Changing the Subject: Women's Discourses and Feminist Theology* (Minneapolis, MN: Fortress Press, 1994), pp. 375–377.

32   For more about truth, see Terrence Tilley, *Story Theology* (Wilmington, DE: Michael Glazier, Inc., 1985), pp. 182–214.

33   This is a very abbreviated version of a larger study in my *Changing the Subject*, pp. 183–238.

34   I have developed "canonical system" from John Frow's work in *Marxism and Literary History* (Oxford: Basil Blackwell, 1989).

35   For a good history of this, see Lois A. Boyd and R. Douglas Brackenridge, *Presbyterian Women in America: Two Centuries of a Quest for Status* (Westport, CT: Greenwood Press, 1983).

36   See Glenna Matthews, *"Just a Housewife": The Rise and Fall of Domesticity in America* (New York, NY: Oxford University Press, 1987).

37   See Michael A. K. Halliday, *Language as Social Semiotic: The Social Interpretation of Language and Meaning* (Baltimore, MD: University Park Press, 1978).

38   The debate here would be between feminists, who claim this is a new formulation, not contained implicitly in the tradition's doctrine of human being, and Lindbeck, who allows new doctrine, but no change to the core. There can be more disruption on the first view.

TWO (OR MORE) KINDS OF SCRIPTURE SCHOLARSHIP

ALVIN PLANTINGA

The serious and scholarly study of the Bible is of first importance for the Christian community. The roll call of those who have pursued this project is maximally impressive: Chrysostom, Augustine, Aquinas, Calvin, Jonathan Edwards and Karl Barth, just for starters. These people and their successors begin from the idea that Scripture is indeed divinely inspired (however exactly they understand this claim); they then try to ascertain the Lord's teaching in the whole of Scripture or (more likely) a given bit. Since the Enlightenment, however, another kind of Scripture scholarship has also come into view. Variously called "higher criticism", "historical criticism", "biblical criticism", or "historical critical scholarship", this variety of Scripture scholarship *brackets* or *prescinds from* what is known by faith and aims to proceed "scientifically", strictly on the basis of reason. I shall call it "Historical Biblical Criticism"—HBC for short. Scripture scholarship of this sort also brackets the belief that the Bible is a special word from the Lord, as well as any other belief accepted on the basis of faith rather than reason.

Now it often happens that the declarations of those who pursue this latter kind are in apparent conflict with the main lines of Christian thought; one who pursues this sort of scholarship is quite unlikely to conclude, for example, that Jesus was really the pre-existent second person of the divine trinity who was crucified, died, and then literally rose from the dead the third day. As Van Harvey says, "So far as the biblical historian is concerned, … there is scarcely a popularly held traditional belief about Jesus that is not regarded with considerable skepticism."[1] I shall try to describe both of these kinds of Scripture scholarship. Then I shall ask the following question: how should a traditional Christian, one who accepts "the great things of the gospel", respond to the deflationary aspects of HBC? How should she think about its

Alvin Plantinga
Department of Philosophy, University of Notre Dame, Notre Dame, IN 46556, USA

apparently corrosive results with respect to traditional Christian belief? I shall argue that she need not be disturbed by the conflict between alleged results of HBC and traditional Christian belief.[2] Indeed, that conflict should not defeat her acceptance of the great things of the gospel—nor, to the degree that those alleged results rest upon epistemological assumptions she does not share, of anything else she accepts on the basis of Biblical teaching.

I. Scripture Divinely Inspired

At millions of worship services every week Christians all over the world hear passages of Scripture and respond by saying, "This is the Word of the Lord." Suppose we begin, therefore, by inquiring into the epistemology of the belief that the Bible is divinely inspired in a special way, and in such a way as to constitute divine discourse. How *does* a Christian come to believe that the gospel of Mark, or the book of Acts, or the entire New Testament is authoritative, because divinely inspired? What (if anything) is the source of its warrant?[3] There are several possibilities. For many, it will be by way of ordinary teaching and testimony. Perhaps I am brought up to believe the Bible is indeed the Word of God (just as I am brought up thinking that thousands perished in the American Civil War), and I have never encountered any reason to doubt this. But an important feature of warrant is that if I accept a belief *B* just on testimony, then *B* has warrant for me only if it had warrant for the testifier as well: the warrant a belief has for the testifiee is derivative from the warrant it has for the testifier.[4] Our question, therefore, becomes this: what is the epistemological status of this belief for those members of the community who do not accept it on the testimony of other members? What is the source of the warrant (if any) this belief has for the Christian community? Well, perhaps a Christian might come to think something like the following:

> Suppose the apostles were commissioned by God through Jesus Christ to be witnesses and representatives (deputies) of Jesus. Suppose that what emerged from their carrying out this commission was a body of apostolic teaching which incorporated what Jesus taught them and what they remembered of the goings-on surrounding Jesus, shaped under the guidance of the Spirit. And suppose that the New Testament books are all either apostolic writings, or formulations of apostolic teaching composed by close associates of one or another apostle. Then it would be correct to construe each book as a medium of divine discourse. And an eminently plausible construal of the process whereby these books found their way into a single canonical text, would be that by way of that process of canonization, God was authorizing these books as together constituting a single volume of divine discourse.[5]

So a Christian might come to think something like the above: she believes
(1) that the apostles were commissioned by God through Jesus Christ to be
witnesses and deputies,
(2) that they produced a body of apostolic teaching which incorporates
what Jesus taught,
and
(3) that the New Testament books are all either apostolic writings or
formulations of apostolic teaching composed by close associates of one or
another apostle.
She also believes
(4) that the process whereby these books found their way into a single
canon is a matter of God's authorizing these books as constituting a single
volume of divine discourse.
She therefore concludes that indeed
(5) the New Testament is a single volume of divine discourse.
But of course our question then would be: how does she know, why does she
believe each of (1)–(4)? What is the source of these beliefs?

Could it be, perhaps, by way of ordinary historical investigation? I doubt
it. The problem is the Principle of Dwindling Probabilities. Suppose a Christian proposes to give a historical argument for the divine inspiration and
consequent authority of the New Testament; and suppose we think of her as
already knowing or believing the central truths of Christianity. She already
knows that there is such a person as God, that the man Jesus is also the divine
Son of God, that through his ministry, passion, death and resurrection we
sinners can have life. These constitute part of her background information,
and can be employed in the historical argument in question. Her body of
background information B with respect to which she estimates the probability of (1)–(4), includes the main lines of Christian teaching. And of course
she knows that the books of the New Testament—some of them, anyway—
apparently teach or presuppose these things. With respect to B, therefore,
perhaps each of (1)–(4) could be considered at least quite plausible and
perhaps even likely to be true.

Still, each is only probable. Perhaps, indeed, each is *very* likely and has a
probability as high as .9 with respect to that body of belief B.[6] Even so, we
can conclude only that the probability of their conjunction, on B, is somewhat
more than .5. In that case, *belief* that the New Testament is the Word of God
would not be appropriate; what would be appropriate is the belief that it is
fairly *likely* that the New Testament is the Word of God. (The probability that
the next throw of this die will not come up either 1 or 2 is greater than .5; that
is nowhere nearly sufficient for my *believing* that it will not come up 1 or 2.)
Of course, we could quibble about these probabilities—no doubt they could
sensibly be thought to be greater than I suggested. No doubt; but they could
also sensibly be thought to be less than I suggested. The historical argument
for (1) to (4) will at best yield probabilities, and at best only a fairly insubstantial

probability of (5) itself. The estimates of the probabilities involved, further-more, will be vague, variable and not really well founded. If the belief in question is to have *warrant* for Christians, its epistemic status for them must be something different from that of a conclusion of ordinary historical in-vestigation.

Now, of course, most Christian communities have taught that the warrant enjoyed by this belief is *not* conferred on it just by way of ordinary historical investigation. The Belgic Confession, one of the most important confessions of the Reformed churches, gives a list (the Protestant list) of the canonical books of the Bible (Article 5); it then goes on:

> And we believe without a doubt all things contained in them—not so much because the church receives them and approves them as such, but above all because the Holy Spirit testifies in our hearts that they are from God, and also because they prove themselves to be from God.

There is a possible ambiguity here; "we believe all things contained in them not so much because the church receives them, but ..."—but to what does this last 'them' refer? The teachings contained in the books, or the books themselves? If the former, then what we have here is the claim that the Holy Spirit is leading us to see, not that a given *book* is from God, but that some *teaching*—e.g., that God in Christ was reconciling the world to himself—is indeed true. If the latter, however, what we would be led to believe is such propositions as *The gospel of John is from God*. I think it is at least fairly clear that the latter is what the Confession intends. According to the Confession, then, there are two sources for the belief that (e.g.) the gospel of John is from God. The first is that the Holy Spirit testifies in our hearts that this book is indeed from God; the Holy Spirit does not merely impel us to believe, with respect to a given teaching of the gospel of John, that it is from God, but also impels us to believe that the gospel of John itself is from God. The second is that the book "proves itself" to be from God. Perhaps here the idea is that the believer first comes to think, with respect to many of the specific teachings of that book, that they are indeed from God; that is, the Holy Spirit causes her to believe this with respect to many of the teachings of the book. She then infers (with the help of other premises) that the whole book has that same status.[7]

This is only *one* way in which this belief could have warrant; there are other possibilities. Perhaps the believer knows by way of the internal in-vitation of the Holy Spirit that the Holy Spirit has guided and preserved the Christian church, making sure that its teachings on important matters are in fact true; then the believer would be warranted in believing, at any rate of those books of the Bible endorsed by all or nearly all traditional Christian communities, that they are from God. Or perhaps, guided by the Holy Spirit, she recapitulates the process whereby the canon was originally formed, pay-ing attention to the original criteria of apostolic authorship, consistency with

apostolic teaching, and the like, and relying on testimony for the propositions such and such books were indeed composed by apostles. There are
also combinations of these ways. However precisely this belief receives its
warrant, then, traditional Christians have accepted the belief that the Bible is
indeed the Word of God and that in it the Lord intends to teach us truths.[8]

II. Traditional Christian Biblical Commentary

Of course, it is not always easy to tell what the Lord *is* teaching us in a given
passage: what he teaches is indeed true, but sometimes it is not clear just
what his teaching is. Part of the problem is the fact that the Bible contains
material of so many different sorts; it is not in this respect like a contemporary book on theology or philosophy. It is not a book full of declarative
sentences, with proper analysis and logical development and all the
accoutrements academics have come to know and love and demand. The Bible
does indeed contain sober assertion; but there is also exhortation, expression
of praise, poetry, the telling of stories and parables, songs, devotional material, history, genealogies, lamentations, confession, prophecy, apocalyptic
material, and much else besides. Some of these (apocalyptic, for example)
present real problems of interpretation (for us, at present): what exactly is
the Lord teaching in Daniel, or Revelation? That is not easy to say.

And even if we stick to straightforward assertion, there are a thousand
questions of interpretation. Here are just a couple of examples. In Matthew
5:17–20, Jesus declares that not a jot or a tittle of the Law shall pass away and
that "... unless your righteousness surpasses that of the Pharisees and the
teachers of the law, you will certainly not enter the kingdom of heaven", but
in Galatians Paul seems to say that observance of the Law does not count for
much; how can we put these together? How do we understand Colossians
1:24: "Now I rejoice in what was suffered for you, and I fill up in my flesh
what is still lacking in regard to Christ's afflictions, for the sake of his body
which is the church"? Is Paul suggesting that Christ's sacrifice is incomplete,
insufficient, that it requires additional suffering on the part of Paul and/or
the rest of us? That seems unlikely. Is it that our suffering can be a *type* of
Christ's, thus standing to the latter in the relation in which a type stands to
the reality it typifies? Or shall we understand it like this: we must distinguish between two kinds of Christ's suffering, the redemptive suffering, the
expiatory and vicarious atonement to which nothing can be added or taken
away, on the one hand, and another kind, also "for the sake of his body",
in which we human beings can genuinely participate? Perhaps it is suffering which can build up, edify the body of Christ, even as our response to
Christ can be deepened by our meditating on Christ's sacrifice for us and
the amazing selfless love displayed in it? Or what? Do Paul and James
contradict each other on the relation between faith and works? Or rather,
since God is the author of Scripture, is he proposing an inconsistent or

self-contradictory teaching for our belief? Well no, surely not, but then how shall we understand the two in relation to each other? More generally, given that God is the principal author of Scripture, how shall we think about the apparent tensions the latter displays?

Scripture, therefore, is indeed inspired: what it teaches is indeed true; but it is not always trivial to tell what it *does* teach. Indeed, many of the sermons and homilies preached in a million churches every Sunday morning are devoted in part to bringing out what might otherwise be obscure in Scriptural teaching. Given that the Bible is a communication from God to humankind, a divine revelation, there is much about it that requires deep and perceptive reflection, much that taxes our best scholarly and spiritual resources. Of course, this fact was not lost on, for example, Chrysostom, Augustine, Aquinas, Calvin, and the others I mentioned earlier on; between them they wrote an impressive number of volumes devoted to powerful reflection on the meaning and teachings of Scripture. (Calvin's commentaries alone run to some twenty-two volumes.) Their aim was to try to determine as accurately as possible just what the Lord proposes to teach us in the Bible. Call this enterprise 'traditional biblical commentary', and note that it displays at least the following three features.

First, Scripture itself is taken to be a wholly authoritative and trustworthy guide to faith and morals; it is authoritative and trustworthy, because it is a revelation from God, a matter of God's speaking to us. Once it is clear, therefore, what the teaching of a given bit of Scripture is, the question of the truth and acceptability of that teaching is settled. In a commentary on Plato, we might decide that what Plato really meant to say was XYZ; we might then go on to consider and evaluate XYZ in various ways, asking whether it is true, or close to the truth, or true in principle, or superseded by things we have learned since Plato wrote, and the like; we might also ask whether Plato's grounds or arguments for XYZ are slight, or acceptable, or substantial, or compelling. These questions are out of place in the kind of Scripture scholarship under consideration. Once convinced that God *is* proposing XYZ for our belief, we do not go on to ask whether it is true, or whether God has made a good case for it. God is not required to make a case.

Secondly, an assumption of the enterprise is that the principal author of the Bible—the entire Bible—is God himself. Of course, each of the books of the Bible has a human author or authors as well; but the principal author is God. This impels us to treat the whole more like a unified communication than a miscellany of ancient books. Scripture is not so much a library of independent books as itself a book with many subdivisions but a central theme: the message of the gospel. By virtue of this unity, furthermore (by virtue of the fact that there is just one principal author), it is possible to "interpret Scripture with Scripture". If a given passage from one of Paul's epistles is puzzling, it is perfectly proper to try to come to clarity as to what God's teaching in this passage is by appealing, not only to what Paul himself says elsewhere in other epistles (his own or others), but also to what is taught elsewhere in Scripture (for example, the gospel of John[9]). Passages in Psalms or Isaiah can be interpreted in terms of the fuller, more explicit disclosure in the New Testament; the serpent elevated on a pole to save the Israelites from disaster can be seen as a type of Christ (and thus as getting some of its significance by way of an implicit reference to Christ, whose being raised on the cross averted a greater disaster for the whole human race). A further consequence: we can quite properly accept propositions that are inferred from premises coming from different parts of the Bible: once we see what God intends to teach in a given passage A and what he intends to teach in a given passage B, we can put the two together, and treat a consequence of these propositions as itself divine teaching.[10]

Thirdly (and connected with the second point), the fact that the principal author of the Bible is God himself means that one cannot always determine the meaning of a given passage by discovering what the human author had in mind. Of course, various post-modern hermeneuticists aim to amuse by telling us that in this case, as in all others, the author's intentions have nothing whatever to do with the meaning of a passage, that the reader herself confers upon it whatever meaning the passage has, or perhaps that even entertaining the idea of a text having meaning is to fall into "hermeneutical innocence"—innocence, oddly enough, which (as they insist) is ineradicably sullied by its inevitable association with oppressive, racist, sexist, homophobic and other offensive modes of thought. This is indeed amusing. Returning to serious business, however, it is obvious (given that the principal author of the Bible is God) that the meaning of a biblical passage will be given by what it is that the Lord intends to teach in that passage, and it is precisely this that biblical commentary tries to discern. Therefore, what the Lord intends to teach us is not identical with what the human author had in mind;[11] the latter may not so much as have thought of what is in fact the teaching of the passage in question. Thus, for example, Christians take the suffering servant passages in Isaiah to be references to Jesus; Jesus himself says (Luke 4:18–21) that the prophecy in Isaiah 61:1–2 is fulfilled in him; John (19:36) takes passages from Exodus, Numbers, Psalms and Zechariah to be references to Jesus and the events of his life and death; Matthew and John take it that Zechariah 9:9 is a reference to Jesus' triumphal entry into Jerusalem (Matthew 21:5 and John 12:15); Hebrews 10 takes passages from Psalms, Jeremiah, and Habakkuk to be references to Christ and events in his career, as does Paul for passages from Psalms and Isaiah in his speech in Acts 13. Indeed, Paul refers to the Old Testament on nearly every page of Romans and both Corinthian epistles, and frequently in other epistles. There is no reason to suppose the human authors of Exodus, Numbers, Psalms, Isaiah, Jeremiah, or Habakkuk had in mind Jesus' triumphal entry, or his incarnation, or other events of Jesus' life and death, or indeed anything else explicitly about Jesus. But the fact that it is God who is the principal author here makes it quite possible that what we are to learn from the text in question is something rather different from what the human author proposed to teach.

III. Historical Biblical Criticism

For at least the last couple of hundred years there has also been a quite different kind of Scripture scholarship variously called "higher criticism", "historical criticism", "biblical criticism", or "historical critical scholarship"; I will call it "historical biblical criticism" (HBC). Clearly, we are indebted to HBC; it has enabled us to learn a great deal about the Bible we otherwise might not have known. Furthermore, some of the methods it has developed can be and have been employed to excellent effect in various studies of interest and importance, including traditional Biblical commentary. It differs importantly from the latter, however. HBC is fundamentally an enlightenment project; it is an effort to try to determine from the standpoint of reason alone what the Scriptural teachings are and whether they are true. Thus HBC eschews the authority and guidance of tradition, magisterium, creed, or any kind of ecclesial or "external" epistemic authority. The idea is to see what can be established (or at least made plausible) using only the light of what we could call "natural, empirical reason". (So, of course, not everyone who uses the methods of textual criticism commonly employed in HBC is involved in the project of HBC as I am thinking of it; to take part in that project one must aim to discover the truth about Scripture and its teachings from the standpoint of reason alone.) The faculties or sources of belief invoked, therefore, would be those that are employed in ordinary history: perception, testimony, reason taken in the sense of *a priori* intuition together with deductive and probabilistic reasoning, Reid's sympathy, by which we discern the thoughts and feelings of another, and so on—but bracketing any proposition one knows by faith or by way of the authority of the church. Spinoza (1632–1677) already lays down the charter for this enterprise: "The rule for [Biblical] interpretation should be nothing but the natural light of reason which is common to all—not any supernatural light nor any external authority."[12]

This project or enterprise is often thought of as part and parcel of the development of modern empirical science, and indeed practitioners of HBC often drape about their shoulders the mantle of modern science. The attraction is not just that HBC can perhaps share in the prestige of modern science, but also that it can share in the obvious epistemic power and excellence of the latter.[13] It is common to think of science itself as our best shot at getting to know what the world is really like; HBC is, among other things, an attempt to apply these widely approved methods to the study of Scripture and the origins of Christianity. Thus Raymond Brown, a Scripture scholar than whom none is more highly respected, believes that HBC is "scientific biblical criticism";[14] it yields "factual results" (p. 9); he intends his own contributions to be "scientifically respectable" (p. 11): and practitioners of HBC investigate the Scriptures with "scientific exactitude" (pp. 18–19).[15]

But what is it, exactly, to study the Bible scientifically? As we will see below there is more than one answer to this question. One theme that seems to command nearly universal assent, however, is that in working at this scientific project (however exactly it is to be understood) you do not invoke or employ any theological assumptions or presuppositions. You do not assume, for example, that the Bible is inspired by God in any special way, or contains anything like specifically divine discourse. You do not assume that Jesus is the divine Son of God, or that he arose from the dead, or that his suffering and death is in some way a propitiatory atonement for human sin, making it possible for us to get once more in the right relationship to God. You do not assume any of these things because in pursuing science, one does not assume or employ any proposition which one knows by faith.[16] (As a consequence, the meaning of a text will be what the human author intended to assert (if it is an assertive kind of text); divine intentions and teaching do not enter into the meaning.[17]) Thus the idea, says E. P. Sanders, is to rely only on "evidence on which everyone can agree".[18] According to Jon Levenson,

> Historical critics thus rightly insist that the tribunal before which interpretations are argued cannot be confessional or 'dogmatic'; the arguments offered must be historically valid, able, that is, to compel the assent of *historians* whatever their religion or lack thereof, whatever their backgrounds, spiritual experiences, or personal beliefs, and without privileging any claim of revelation.[19]

Barnabas Lindars explains that

> There are in fact two reasons why many scholars are very cautious about miracle stories … The second reason is historical. The religious literature of the ancient world is full of miracle stories, and we cannot believe them all. It is not open to a scholar to decide that, just because he is a believing Christian, he will accept all the Gospel miracles at their face value, but at the same time he will repudiate miracles attributed to Isis. All such accounts have to be scrutinized with equal detachment.[20]

And even Luke Timothy Johnson, who is in general astutely critical of HBC:

> It is obviously important to study Christian origins historically. And in such historical inquiry, faith commitments should play no role. Christianity is no more privileged for the historian than any other human phenomenon.[21]

In practice, this emphasis means that HBC tends to deal especially with questions of *composition* and *authorship*, these being the questions most easily addressed by the methods employed. When was the document in question composed—or more exactly, since we cannot assume that we are dealing with a single unified document here, when were its various parts composed? How was the gospel of Luke, for example, composed? Was it written by one person, relying on his memory of Jesus and his words and deeds, or was it assembled from various reports, alleged quotations, songs, poems and the like in the oral tradition? Was it dependent on one or more earlier written or oral sources? Why did the editor or redactor put the book together in just the way he did—was it to make a theological point in a current controversy? Where traditional Biblical commentary assumes that the entire Bible is really one book with a single principal author, HBC tends to give us a collection of books by many authors. And even within the confines of a single book, it may give us a collection of discontinuous sayings and episodes (pericopes), these having been stitched together by one or more redactors. How much of what is reported as the sayings and discourse of Jesus really was said by Jesus? Can we discern various strata in the book—perhaps a bottom stratum, including the actual sayings of Jesus himself, and then successive overlaying strata? As Robert Alter says, scholarship of this kind tends to be "excavative"; the idea is to dig behind the document as we actually have it to see what can be determined of its history.[22]

Of course, the idea is also to see, as far as this is possible, whether the events reported—in the gospels, for example—really happened, and whether the picture they give of Jesus is in fact historically accurate. Did he say the things they say he said, and do the things they say he did? Here the assumption is that we cannot simply take at face value the gospels as we now have them. There may have been all sorts of additions and subtractions and alterations made in the interest of advancing theological points. Further, the New Testament books are written from the standpoint of faith—faith that Jesus really was the Christ, did indeed suffer and die and rise from the dead, and did accomplish our salvation. From the standpoint of reason alone, however, this faith must be bracketed; hence (from that standpoint) the hermeneutics of suspicion is appropriate here. (This suspicion is sometimes carried so far that it reminds one of the way in which the CIA's denial that Mr X is a spy is taken as powerful evidence that Mr X is indeed a spy.)

A. Varieties of HBC

Those who practice HBC, therefore, propose to proceed without employing theological assumptions or anything one knows by faith (if indeed there is anything one knows by faith); these things are to be bracketed. Instead, one proceeds scientifically, on the basis of reason alone. Beyond this, however, there is vastly less concord. What is to count as reason? Precisely what premises can be employed in an argument from reason alone? What exactly does it mean to proceed scientifically?

1. Troeltschian HBC

Here many contemporary biblical critics will appeal to the thought and teaching of Ernst Troeltsch.[23] Thus John Collins:

> Among theologians these principles received their classic formulation from Ernst Troeltsch in 1898. Troeltsch sets out three principles ...: (1) The principle of criticism or methodological doubt: since any conclusion is subject to revision, historical inquiry can never attain absolute certainty but only relative degrees of probability. (2) The principle of analogy: historical knowledge is possible because all events are similar in principle. We must assume that the laws of nature in biblical times were the same as now. Troeltsch referred to this as 'the almighty power of analogy.' (3) The principle of correlation: the phenomena of history are inter-related and inter-dependent and no event can be isolated from the sequence of historical cause and effect.[24]

Collins adds a fourth principle, this one taken from Van Harvey's *The Historian and the Believer*,[25] a more recent *locus classicus* for the proper method of historical criticism:

> To these should be added the principle of autonomy, which is indispensable for any critical study. Neither church nor state can prescribe for the scholar which conclusions should be reached. (*loc. cit.*)

Now the first thing to note is that each of these principles is multiply ambiguous. In particular, each (except perhaps for the second) has a non-controversial, indeed, platitudinous interpretation. The first principle seems to be a *comment on* historical inquiry rather than a principle for its practice: historical inquiry can never attain absolutely certain results. (Perhaps the implied methodological principle is that in doing historical criticism, you should avoid claiming absolute certainty for your results.) Fair enough, I suppose nearly everyone would agree that few historical results of any significance are as certain as, say, that $2 + 1 = 3$, but if so, they do not achieve absolute certainty. (The only reasonably plausible candidates for historical events that *are* absolutely certain, I suppose, would be such 'historical' claims as that either Caesar crossed the Rubicon or else he did not.)

The third also has a platitudinous interpretation. What Troeltsch says is, "The sole task of history in its specifically theoretical aspect is to explain every movement, process, state and nexus of things by reference to the web of its causal relations."[26] This too can be seen as toothless if not platitudinous. Every event is to be explained by reference to the web of its causal relations—which of course would also include the intentions and actions of persons. Well then, consider even such an event as the resurrection of Jesus from the dead: according to the principle at hand, this event too would have to be explained by reference to the web of its causal relations. No problem; on the traditional view, this event was caused by God himself, who caused it in order to achieve certain of his aims and ends, in particular making it possible for human beings to be reconciled with God. So taken, this principle would exclude very little.

I say the second principle is perhaps the exception to the claim that each has a banal, uncontroversial interpretation: that is because on any plausible interpretation the second principle seems to entail the existence of *natural laws*. That there *are* such things as natural laws was a staple of 17th and 18th century science and philosophy of science;[27] what science discovers (so they thought) is just these laws of nature.[28] Empiricists have always been dubious about natural laws, however, and at present the claim that there are any such things is at best extremely controversial.[29]

So all but one of Troeltsch's principles have platitudinous interpretations; but these are not in fact the interpretations given to them in the community of HBC. Within that community those principles are understood in such a way as to preclude *direct divine action* in the world. Not that all in this community *accept* Troeltsch's principles in their nonplatitudinous interpretation; rather, those who think of themselves as accepting (or rejecting) those principles think of themselves as accepting or rejecting their nonplatitudinous versions. (Presumably *everyone* accepts them taken platitudinously.) So taken, these principles imply that God has not in fact specially inspired any human authors in such a way that what they write is really divine speech addressed to us; nor has he raised Jesus from the dead, or turned water into wine, or performed miracles of any other sorts.

Thus Rudolph Bultmann:

> The historical method includes the presupposition that history is a unity in the sense of a closed continuum of effects in which individual events are connected by the succession of cause and effect.

This continuum, furthermore,

> cannot be rent by the interference of supernatural, transcendent powers.[30]

Many other theologians, oddly enough, chime in with agreement: God cannot or at any rate would not and will not act directly in the world. Thus John Macquarrie:

> The way of understanding miracles that appeals to breaks in the natural order and to supernatural intervention belongs to the mythological outlook and cannot commend itself in a post-mythological climate of thought ... The traditional conception of miracle is irreconcilable with our modern understanding of both science and history. Science proceeds on the assumption that whatever events occur in the world can be accounted for in terms of other events that also belong within the world; and if on some occasions we are unable to give a complete account of some happening ... the scientific conviction is that further research will bring to

light further factors in the situation, but factors that will turn out to be just as immanent and this-worldly as those already known.[31]

And Langdon Gilkey:

> ... contemporary theology does not expect, nor does it speak of, wondrous divine events on the surface of natural and historical life. The causal nexus in space and time which the Enlightenment science and philosophy introduced into the Western mind ... is also assumed by modern theologians and scholars; since they participate in the modern world of science both intellectually and existentially, they can scarcely do anything else. Now this assumption of a causal order among pheno-menal events, and therefore of the authority of the scientific interpreta-tion of observable events, makes a great difference to the validity one assigns to biblical narratives and so to the way one understands their meaning. Suddenly a vast panoply of divine deeds and events recorded in scripture are no longer regarded as having actually happened .... Whatever the Hebrews believed, *we* believe that the biblical people lived in the same causal continuum of space and time in which we live, and so one in which no divine wonders transpired and no divine voices were heard.[32]

Gilkey says no divine wonders have transpired and no divine voices have been heard; Macquarrie adds that in this post-mythological age, we cannot brook the idea of "breaks in the natural order and supernatural interven-tion". Each, therefore, is ruling out the possibility of miracle, including the possibility of special divine action in inspiring human authors in such a way that what they write constitutes an authoritative communication from God. Now, of course, it is far from easy to say just what a miracle is; this topic is connected with deep and thorny questions about occasionalism, natural law, natural potentialities, and so on. We need not get into all that, however. The Troeltschian idea is that there is a certain way in which things ordinarily go; there are certain regularities, whether or not due to natural law, and God can be counted on to act in such a way as never to abrogate those regularities. Of course, God *could* if he chose abrogate those regularities (after all, even those natural laws, if there are any, are his creatures); but we can be sure, some-how, that God will not abrogate those regularities. Troeltschian Scripture scholarship, therefore, will proceed on the basis of the assumption that God never does anything specially; in particular, he neither raised Jesus from the dead nor specially inspired the Biblical authors.

2. Duhemian HBC

Not all who accept and practice HBC accept Troeltsch's principles, and we can see another variety of HBC by thinking about an important suggestion made by Pierre Duhem. Duhem was both a serious Catholic and a serious scientist; he was accused (as he thought) by Abel Rey[33] of allowing his religious and metaphysical views as a Christian to enter his physics in an improper way. Duhem repudiated this suggestion, claiming that his Christianity did not enter his physics in any way at all and *a fortiori* did not enter it in an improper way.[34] Furthermore, the *correct* or *proper* way to pursue physical theory, he said, was the way in which he had in fact done it; physical theory should be completely independent of religious or metaphysical views or commitments.

Why did he think so? What did he have against metaphysics? Here he strikes a characteristic Enlightenment note: if you think of metaphysics as ingressing into physics, he says, then your estimate of the worth of a physical theory will depend upon the metaphysics you adopt. Physical theory will be dependent upon metaphysics in such a way that someone who does not accept the metaphysics involved in a given physical theory cannot accept the physical theory either. And the problem with *that* is that the disagreements that run riot in metaphysics will ingress into physics, so that the latter cannot be an activity we can all work at together, regardless of our metaphysical views:

> Now to make physical theories depend on metaphysics is surely not the way to let them enjoy the privilege of universal consent … If theoretical physics is subordinated to metaphysics, the divisions separating the diverse metaphysical systems will extend into the domain of physics. A physical theory reputed to be satisfactory by the sectarians of one metaphysical school will be rejected by the partisans of another school. (Duhem, p. 10)

Duhem's main point, I think, is that if a physical theorist employs metaphysical assumptions or other notions that are not accepted by other workers in the field, and employs them in such a way that those who do not accept them cannot accept his physical theory, then to that extent his work cannot be accepted by those others; to that extent, furthermore, the cooperation important to science will be compromised. He therefore proposes a conception of science (or physics in particular) according to which the latter is independent of metaphysics:

> … I have denied metaphysical doctrines the right to testify for or against any physical theory. … Whatever I have said of the method by which physics proceeds, or the nature and scope that we must attribute to the theories it constructs, does not in any way prejudice either the metaphysical doctrines or religious beliefs of anyone who accepts my words. The believer and the nonbeliever may both work in common accord for the progress of physical science such as I have tried to define it. (Ibid., pp. 274–275)

Duhem's proposal, reduced to essentials, is that physicists should not make essential use of religious or metaphysical assumptions in doing their physics: in that way lies chaos and cacophony, as each of the warring sects does things its own way. If we want to have the sort of commonality and genuine dialogue that promotes progress in physics, we should avoid assumptions —metaphysical, religious or otherwise—that are not accepted by all parties to the discussion.[35]

Duhem's suggestion is interesting and important, and (although Duhem himself did not do so) can obviously be applied far beyond the confines of physical theory: for example, to Scripture scholarship. Suppose we say that *Duhemian* Scripture scholarship is Scripture scholarship that does not involve any theological, religious or metaphysical assumptions that are not accepted by everyone in the relevant community.[36] Thus the Duhemian Scripture scholar would not take for granted either that God is the principal author of the Bible or that the main lines of the Christian story are in fact true; these are not accepted by all who are party to the discussion. She would not take for granted that Jesus rose from the dead, or that any other miracle has occurred; she could not so much as take it for granted that miracles are possible, since these claims are rejected by many who are party to the discussion. On the other hand, of course, Duhemian Scripture scholarship cannot take it for granted that Christ did *not* rise from the dead or that *no* miracles have occurred, or that miracles are *im*possible. Nor, of course, could it employ Troeltsch's principles (taken non-platitudinously); not everyone accepts them. Duhemian Scripture scholarship fits well with Sanders' suggestion that "what is needed is more secure evidence, evidence on which everyone can agree" (above, p. 251). It also fits well with John Meier's fantasy of "an unpapal conclave" of Jewish, Catholic, Protestant and agnostic scholars, locked in the basement of the Harvard Divinity School library until they come to consensus on what historical methods can show about the life and mission of Jesus.[37] Among the proposed benefits of Duhemian HBC, obviously, are just the benefits Duhem cites: people of very different religious and theological beliefs can cooperate in this enterprise. Furthermore, although in principle the traditional Biblical commentator and the Troeltschian Biblical scholar could discover whatever is unearthed by Duhemian means, it is in fact likely that much will be learned in this cooperative enterprise that would not be learned by either group working alone.

3. Spinozistic HBC

Troeltschian and Duhemian HBC do not exhaust HBC; one can be a practitioner of HBC and accept neither. You might propose to follow reason alone in Scripture scholarship, but think that the Troeltschian principles, taken in the strong version in which they imply that God never acts specially in the world, are not in fact deliverances of reason. Reason alone, you say, certainly cannot demonstrate that God never acts specially in the world, or that no miracles have ever occurred. If so, you would not be a Troeltschian. On the other hand, you might also reject Duhemianism as well: for you might think that, as a matter of fact, there are deliverances of reason not accepted by everyone party to the project of Scripture scholarship. (The deliverances of reason are indeed *open* to all, but impeding factors of one kind or another can sometimes prevent someone from seeing the truth of one or another of them.) But then you might yourself employ those deliverances of reason in pursuing Scripture scholarship, thereby employing assumptions not accepted by everyone involved in the project, and thereby rejecting Duhemianism. You might therefore propose to follow reason alone, but be neither a Troeltschian nor a Duhemian. Suppose we use the term 'Spinozistic HBC'[38] to denote this variety of HBC. The Spinozist concurs with the Troeltschian and Duhemian that no theological assumptions or beliefs are to be employed in HBC. She differs from the Troeltschian in paying the same compliment to Troeltsch's principles: they too are not deliverances of reason and hence are not to be employed in HBC. And she differs from the Duhemian in holding that there are some deliverances of reason not accepted by all who are party to the project of Scripture scholarship; hence, she proposes to employ some propositions or beliefs rejected by the Duhemian.

A final point: It is not of course accurate to suppose that all who practice HBC fall neatly into one or another of these categories. There are all sorts of half-way houses, lots of haltings between two opinions, many who fall partly into one and partly into another, and many who have never clearly seen that there *are* these categories. A real live Scripture scholar may be unlikely to have spent a great deal of thought on the epistemological foundations of his or her discipline and is likely to straddle one or more of the categories I mention.

B. Tensions with Traditional Christianity

There has been a history of substantial tension between HBC and traditional Christians. Thus David Friedrich Strauss[39] in 1835: "Nay, if we would be candid with ourselves, that which was once sacred history for the Christian believer is, for the enlightened portion of our contemporaries, only fable." Of course, the unenlightened faithful were not so unenlightened that they failed to notice this feature of Biblical criticism. Writing ten years after the publication of Strauss's book, William Pringle complains that, "In Germany, Biblical criticism is almost a national pursuit ... Unhappily, [the critics] were but too frequently employed in maintaining the most dangerous errors, in opposing every inspired statement which the mind of man is unable fully to comprehend, in divesting religion of its spiritual and heavenly character, and in undermining the whole fabric of revealed truth."[40]

Perhaps among Pringle's complaints were the following. First, practitioners of HBC tend to treat the Bible as a set of separate books rather than a unified communication from God. Thus, they tend to reject the idea that Old Testament passages can be properly understood as making reference to Jesus Christ, or to events in his life: "Critical scholars rule out clairvoyance as an explanation axiomatically. Instead of holding that the Old Testament predicts events in the life of Jesus, critical scholars of the New Testament say that each Gospel writer sought to exploit Old Testament passages in order to bolster his case for the messianic and dominical claims of Jesus or of the church on his behalf."[41] More generally, Brevard Childs: "For many decades the usual way of initiating entering students in the Bible was slowly to dismantle the church's traditional teachings regarding scripture by applying the acids of criticism."[42]

Second, following Ernst Troeltsch HBC tends to discount miracle stories, taking it as axiomatic that miracles do not and did not really happen, or at any rate claiming that the proper method for HBC cannot admit miracles either as evidence or conclusions. Perhaps Jesus effected cures of some psychosomatic disorders, but nothing that modern medical science cannot explain. Many employing this method propose that Jesus never thought of himself as divine, or as the Messiah, or as capable of forgiving sin[43]—let alone as having died and then risen from the dead. "The Historical Jesus researchers," says Luke Timothy Johnson, "insist that the 'real Jesus' must be found in the facts of his life before his death. The resurrection is, when considered at all, seen in terms of visionary experience, or as a continuation of an 'empowerment' that began before Jesus' death. Whether made explicit or not, the operative premise is that there is no 'real Jesus' after his death" (Johnson, p. 144).

Those who follow these methods sometimes produce quite remarkable accounts—and accounts remarkably different from traditional Christian understanding. According to Barbara Thiering's *Jesus and the Riddle of the Dead Sea Scrolls*,[44] for example, Jesus was buried in a cave; he did not actually die and was revived by the magician Simon Magus, whereupon he married Mary Magdalene, settled down, fathered three children, was divorced and finally died in Rome. According to Morton Smith, Jesus was a practicing homosexual and conjurer.[45] According to German Scripture scholar Gerd Ludemann: the Resurrection is "an empty formula that must be rejected by anyone holding a scientific world view".[46] G. A. Wells goes so far as to claim that our name 'Jesus', as it turns up in the Bible, is empty: like 'Santa Claus', it does not trace back to or denote anyone at all.[47] John Allegro apparently thinks there was no such person as Jesus of Nazareth; Christianity began as a hoax designed to fool the Romans, and preserve the cult of a certain hallucinogenic mushroom (*Amanita muscaria*). Still, the name 'Christ' is not empty: it is really a name of that mushroom.[48] As engaging a claim as any is that Jesus, while neither merely legendary, nor actually a mushroom, was in fact an atheist, the first Christian atheist.[49] And even if we set aside the lunatic fringe, Van Harvey is correct: "So far as the biblical historian is concerned, ... there is scarcely a popularly held traditional belief about Jesus that is not regarded with considerable skepticism" (NTS, p. 193).

IV. Why Are Not Most Christians More Concerned?

So HBC has not in general been sympathetic to traditional Christian belief; it has hardly been an encouragement to the faithful. But the faithful seem relatively unconcerned; of course, they find traditional biblical commentary of great interest and importance, but the beliefs and attitudes of HBC have not seemed to filter down to them, despite its dominance in mainline seminaries. According to Van Harvey, "Despite decades of research, the average person tends to think of the life of Jesus in much the same terms as Christians did three centuries ago ..." Harvey finds this puzzling: "Why is it that, in a culture so dominated by experts in every field, the opinion of New Testament historians has had so little influence on the public?" (Ibid., p. 194). Are traditional Christians just ignoring inconvenient evidence? In what follows I will try to answer these questions. Obviously, HBC has contributed greatly to our knowledge of the Bible, in particular the circumstances and conditions of its composition; it has given us new alternatives as to how to understand the human authors, and this has also given us new ideas as to how to understand the divine Author. Nevertheless, there are in fact excellent reasons for tending to ignore that "considerable skepticism", of which Harvey speaks. I do not mean to claim that the ordinary person in the pew ignores it because she has these reasons clearly in mind; no doubt she does not. I say only that these reasons are *good reasons* for a traditional Christian to ignore the deflationary results of HBC.

What might these reasons be? Well of course one thing is that skeptical Scripture scholars display vast disagreement among themselves.[50] There is also the fact that quite a number of the arguments they propose seem at best wholly inconclusive. Perhaps the endemic vice or at any rate the perennial temptation of HBC is what we might call the Fallacy of Creeping Certitude. To practice this fallacy, you note that some proposition A is probable (to .9, say) with respect to your background knowledge k (what you know to be true); you therefore annex it to k. Then you note that a proposition B is probable with respect to k&A; you therefore annex it too to k. Then you note that C is probable to .9 with respect to A&B&k, and also annex it to K; similarly for (say) D, E, F and G. You then pronounce A&B&C&D&E&F&G highly probable with respect to k, our evidence. But the fact is (as we learn from the probability calculus) that these probabilities must be *multiplied*—so that in fact the probability of A&B&C&D&E&F&G is .9 to the 7th power, i.e., less than .5! But suppose we look into reasons or arguments for preferring the results of HBC to those of traditional commentary. Why should we suppose that the former take us closer to the truth than the latter? Troeltsch's principles are particularly important here. As understood in the interpretative community of HBC, they preclude special divine action including special divine inspiration of Scripture and the occurrence of miracles. As Gilkey says, "Suddenly a vast panoply of divine deeds and events recorded in scripture are no longer regarded as having actually happened" (above, p. 255). Many academic theologians and Scripture scholars appear to believe that Troeltschian HBC is *de rigueur*; it is often regarded as the only intellectually respectable variety of Scripture scholarship, or the only variety that has any claim to the mantle of science. (And many who arrive at relatively traditional conclusions in Scripture scholarship nevertheless pay at least lip service to the Troeltschian ideal, somehow feeling in a semi-confused way that this is the epistemically respectable or privileged way of proceeding.) But why think Scripture scholarship should proceed in this specific way—as opposed both to traditional biblical commentary and varieties of HBC that do not accept Troeltsch's principles? Are there any reasons or arguments for those principles?

A. Force Majeure

If so, they are extraordinarily well hidden. One common suggestion, however, seems to be a sort of appeal to *force majeure*: we simply cannot help it. Given our historical position, there is nothing else we can do; we are all in the grip of historical forces beyond our control (this thing is bigger than either one of us). This reaction is typified by those, who like Harvey, Macquarrie, Gilkey, and others claim that nowadays, given our cultural situation, we just do not have any options. There are potent historical forces that impose these ways of thinking upon us; like it or not, we are blown about by these powerful winds of doctrine. "The causal nexus in space and time which the Enlightenment science and philosophy introduced into the Western mind ... is also assumed by modern theologians and scholars; since they participate in the modern world of science both intellectually and existentially, they can scarcely do anything else", says Gilkey (above, p. 255); another example is Bultmann's famous remark to the effect that "it is impossible to use electrical light and the wireless and to avail ourselves of modern medical and surgical discoveries, and at the same time to believe in the New Testament world of spirits and miracles."[51]

But is not this view—that we are all compelled by contemporary historical forces to hold the sort of view in question—historically naive? First, why think we proceed together in lockstep through history, all at any given time perforce holding the same views and making the same assumptions? Clearly we do not do any such thing. The contemporary intellectual world is much more like a horse race (or perhaps a demolition derby) than a triumphal procession, more like a battleground than a Democratic Party fund-raiser, where everyone can be counted on to support the same slate. At present, for example, there are many like Macquarrie, Harvey and Gilkey who accept the semi-deistic view that God (if there is any such person) could not or would not act miraculously in history. But this is not, of course, the view of nearly everyone at present; hundreds of millions would reject it. The fact is that far more people reject this view than accept it. (So even if Gilkey, *et al.*, were right about the inevitable dance of history, they would be wrong in their elitist notion to the effect that what *they* do is the current step.)

The utter obviousness of this fact suggests a second interpretation of this particular justification of Troeltschian HBC. Perhaps what the apologists really mean is not that *everyone* nowadays accepts this semi-deism (that is trivially false), but that everyone *in the know* does. Everyone who is properly educated and has read his Kant and Hume (and Troeltsch) and reflected on the meaning of the wireless and electric light knows these things; as for the rest of humanity (including, I suppose, those of us who have read our Kant and Hume but are unimpressed), their problem is simple ignorance. Perhaps people generally do not march lockstep through history, but those in the know do; and right now they all or nearly all reject special divine action.

But even if we chauvinistically stick to educated Westerners, this is still doubtful *in excelsis*. "The traditional conception of miracle", Macquarrie says, "is irreconcilable with *our* modern understanding of both science and history" (above, p. 254; emphasis added): to whom does this 'our', here refer? To those who have gone to university, are well-educated, know at least a little science, and have thought about the bearing of these matters on the possibility of miracles? If so, the claim is once more whoppingly false. Very many well-educated people (including even some theologians) understand science and history in a way that is entirely compatible both with the possibility and with the actuality of miracles. Many physicists and engineers understand "electrical light and the wireless" vastly better than Bultmann or his contemporary followers, but nonetheless hold precisely those New Testament beliefs Bultmann thinks incompatible with using electric lights and radios. There are large numbers of educated contemporaries (including even some with Ph.Ds!) who believe Jesus really and literally arose from the dead, that God performs miracles in the contemporary world, and even that there are both demons and spirits who are active in the contemporary world. As a matter of historical fact, there are any number of contemporaries, and contemporary intellectuals very well acquainted with science, who do not feel any problem at all in pursuing science and also believing in miracles, angels, Christ's resurrection, the lot.

Once more, however, Macquarrie, *et al.*, must know this as well as anyone else; so what do he and his friends really mean? How can they make these claims about what 'we'[52]—we who use the products of science and know a bit about it—can and cannot believe? How can they blithely exclude or ignore the thousands, indeed millions of contemporary Christians who do not think as they do? The answer must be that they think those Christians somehow do not count. What they really mean to say, I fear, is that they and their friends think this way, and anyone who demurs is so ignorant as to be properly ignored. But that is at best a bit slim as a *reason* for accepting the Troeltschian view; it is more like a nasty little piece of arrogance. Nor is it any better for being tucked away in the suggestion that somehow we just cannot help ourselves. Of course, it is possible that Gilkey and his friends cannot help themselves; in that case they can hardly be blamed for accepting the view in question.[53] This incapacity on their parts, however, is no recommendation of Troeltsch's principles.

So this is at best a poor reason for thinking serious Biblical scholarship must be Troeltschian. Is there a better reason? A second suggestion, perhaps connected with the plea of inability to do otherwise, is given by the suggestion that the very practice of science presupposes rejection of the idea of miracle or special divine action in the world. "Science proceeds on the assumption that whatever events occur in the world can be accounted for in terms of other events that also belong within the world", says Macquarrie (above, p. 254); perhaps he means to suggest that the very practice of science requires that one reject (e.g.) the idea of God's raising someone from the dead. Of course, the argument form

if X were true, it would be inconvenient for science; therefore, X is false

is at best moderately compelling. We are not just given that the Lord has arranged the universe for the comfort and convenience of the American Academy of Science. To think otherwise is to be like the drunk who insisted on looking for his lost car keys under the streetlight, on the grounds that the light was better there. (In fact it would be to go the drunk one better: it would be to insist that since the keys would be hard to find in the dark, they must be under the light.)

But why think in the first place that we would have to embrace this semideism in order to do science?[54] Newton certainly did some sensible science, but he thought Jesus was raised from the dead, as do many contemporary physicists. But of course that is physics; perhaps the problem would be (as Bultmann suggests) with *medicine*. Is the idea that one could not do medical research, or prescribe medications, if one thought that God has done miracles in the past and might even occasionally do some nowadays? To put the suggestion explicitly is to refute it; there is not the faintest reason why I could not sensibly believe that God raised Jesus from the dead and also engage in medical research into, say, Usher's Syndrome or Multiple Sclerosis, or into ways of staving off the ravages of coronary disease. What would be the problem? That it is always *possible* that God should do something different, thus spoiling my experiment? But that *is* possible: God is omnipotent. (Or do we have here a new antitheistic argument? If God exists, he could spoil my experiment; but nothing can spoil my experiment; therefore ...) No doubt if I thought God *often* or *usually* did things in an idiosyncratic way, so that there really are not much by way of discoverable regularities to be found, *then* perhaps I could not sensibly engage in scientific research; the latter presupposes a certain regularity, predictability, stability in the world. But that is an entirely different matter. What I must assume in order to do science, is only that *ordinarily* and for the *most* part these regularities hold.[55] This reason, too, then, is monumentally insufficient as a reason for holding that we are somehow obliged to accept the principles underlying Troeltschian Biblical scholarship.

It is therefore difficult indeed to see any reason for supposing that Troeltschian Scripture scholarship is somehow *de rigueur* or somehow forced upon us by our history.

B. A Moral Imperative?

Van Harvey proposes another reason for pursuing Troeltschian scholarship and preferring it to traditional Biblical commentary;[56] his reason is broadly *moral* or *ethical*. He begins[57] by referring to a fascinating episode in Victorian intellectual history[58] in which certain Victorian intellectuals found themselves wrestling with a serious problem of intellectual integrity. As Harvey sees it, they "believed that it was morally reprehensible to insist that these claims [Christian claims about the activities and teachings of Jesus] were true on faith while at the same time arguing that they were also the legitimate objects of historical inquiry" (Harvey, NTS, p. 195). Now I think this is a tendentious account of the problem these intellectuals faced—tendentious, because it makes it look as if these intellectuals were endorsing, with unerring prescience, precisely the position Harvey himself proposes to argue for. The fact is, I think, their position was both less idiosyncratic and far more plausible. After all, why should anyone think it immoral to believe by faith what could also be investigated by other sources of belief or knowledge? I am curious about your whereabouts last Friday night: were you perhaps at The Linebacker's Bar? Perhaps I could find out in three different ways: by asking you, by asking your wife, and by examining the bar for your fingerprints (fortunately the bar is never washed). Would there be something immoral in using one of these methods when in fact the others were also available? That is not easy to believe.

It was not just *that* that troubled the Victorians. Had they been confident that both faith and historical investigation were reliable avenues to the truths in question, they surely would not have thought it immoral to believe on the basis of one of these as opposed to the other or both. Their problem was deeper. They were troubled (among other things) by the German Scripture scholarship about which they knew relatively little; but they did know enough to think (rightly or wrongly) that it posed a real threat to the Christian beliefs that for many of them were in any event already shaky. They suspected or feared that this Scripture scholarship could show or would show or already had shown that essential elements of the Christian faith were just false. They were also troubled by what many saw as the antisupernaturalistic and antitheistic bent of science: could one really believe in the New Testament world of spirits and miracles in the era of the steam engine and ocean liner? They were troubled by the advent of Darwinism, which seemed to many to contradict the Christian picture of human origins. They were convinced, following Locke and the whole classical foundationalist tradition, that the right way to hold beliefs on these topics is by following the (propositional) evidence wherever it leads; and they were deeply worried about where this evidence was in fact leading. They were troubled, in short, by a variety of factors all of which seemed to suggest that traditional Christian belief was really no more than a beautiful story: inspiring, uplifting, perhaps necessary to public morality, but just a story. Given our scientific coming of age, they feared, informed people would regretfully have to jettison traditional Christian belief, perhaps (especially on ceremonial occasions) with an occasional nostalgic backward look.

But many of them also longed for the comfort and security of serious Christian belief; to lose it was like being thrown out of our Father's house into a hostile or indifferent world. And, of course, many of the Victorians had strong moral opinions and a highly developed moral sense. They thought it weak, spineless, cowardly to refuse to face these specters, to hide them from oneself, to engage in self-deception and double-think. All of this, they thought, is unworthy of a serious and upright person. They abhorred the weakness and moral softness of the sort of stance in which you suspect the bitter truth, but refuse to investigate the matter, preferring to hide the truth from yourself, perhaps hoping it will somehow go away. Many of them thought this was precisely what some of the clergy and other educators were doing, and despised them for it. Far better to face the sad truth with intellectual honesty, manly courage and a stiff upper lip. So it was not just that they thought it reprehensible to believe on faith what can also be addressed by reason or historical investigation. It was rather that they suspected and deeply feared that the latter (together with the other factors I mentioned) would undermine the former. And they scorned and detested a sort of willful head-in-the-sand attitude in which, out of timidity or fear or a desire for comfort, one refuses to face the facts. It is reasons such as these that account for the moral fervor (if not stridency) of W. K. Clifford's oft-anthologized "The Ethics of Belief".[59]

However things may have stood with the Victorians, Harvey proposes the following bit of moral dogma:

The gulf separating the conservative Christian believer and the New Testament scholar can be seen as the conflict between two antithetical ethics of belief ... New Testament scholarship is now so specialized and requires so much preparation that the layperson has simply been disqualified from having any right to a judgment regarding the truth or falsity of certain historical claims. Insofar as the conservative Christian believer is a layperson who has no knowledge of the New Testament scholarship, he or she is simply not entitled to certain historical beliefs at all. Just as the average layperson is scarcely in a position to have an informed judgment about the seventh letter of Plato, the relationship of Montezuma to Cortez, or the authorship of the Donation of Constantine, so the average layperson has no right to an opinion about the authorship of the Fourth Gospel or the trustworthiness of the synoptics (Harvey, NTS, p. 197).

"The layperson has simply been disqualified from having any right to a judgment regarding the truth or falsity of certain historical claims. ..." Strong words! In an earlier age, priests and ministers, often the only educated members of their congregations, would exercise a certain intellectual and spiritual leadership, hoping the flock would in fact come to see, appreciate, and of course believe the truth. On Harvey's showing, the flock does not so much as have a right to an opinion on these points—not even an opinion purveyed by the experts! Harvey complains that many students seem unreceptive to the results of Scripture scholarship (Harvey, NTS, p. 193). But of course if he is right, the students do not have a right to believe the results of Scripture scholarship; they are therefore doing no more than their simple duty in refusing to believe them. One hopes Harvey remembers, when teaching his classes, not to put his views on these matters in an attractive and winsome fashion—after all, if he did so, some of the students might *believe* them, in which case they would be sinning and he himself would be giving offense in the Pauline sense (Romans 14, not to mention I Cor. 8:9).

But suppose we sadly avert our gaze from this elitism run amok: why does Harvey think that only the historian has a right to hold an opinion on these matters? Clearly enough, because he thinks that the only way to achieve accurate and reliable information on these matters is by way of Troeltschian scholarship. And *that* opinion, obviously, presupposes the philosophical and theological opinion that there is not any *other* epistemic avenue to these matters; it presupposes that, for example, faith (and the internal instigation or testimony of the Holy Spirit) is not a source of warranted belief or knowledge on these topics. If the latter *were* a source of warranted belief, and if the "average layperson" had access to this source (if the "average layperson" could have faith), then presumably there would be nothing whatever wrong with her holding views on these matters on this basis. "Just as the average layperson is scarcely in a position to have an informed judgment about the seventh letter of Plato, the relationship of Montezuma to Cortez, or the authorship of the Donation of Constantine, so the average layperson has no right to an opinion about the authorship of the Fourth Gospel or the trustworthiness of the synoptics," says Harvey. The only way to determine the truth about the seventh letter of Plato is by way of ordinary historical investigation; the same goes, Harvey assumes, for questions about the life and ministry of Christ, whether he rose from the dead, whether he thought of himself as a Messiah, and the like. What lies at the bottom of this moral claim is really a philosophical/theological judgment: that traditional Christian belief is completely mistaken in taking it that faith is in fact a reliable source of true and warranted belief on these topics.

This view is not, of course, a result of historical scholarship, Troeltschian or otherwise; nor is it supported by arguments that will appeal to anyone who does not already agree with him—or indeed by any arguments at all. Harvey's view is rather a *presupposition*, a methodological prescription of the pursuit of Troeltschian historical criticism and proscription of traditional Biblical commentary. So it can hardly be thought of as an independent good reason for preferring the former to the latter. What we have are different philosophical/theological positions that dictate different ways of pursuing Scripture scholarship. A way to show that the one really *is* superior to the other would be to give a good argument *for* the one philosophical/theological position, or *against* the other. Harvey does neither, simply assuming (uncritically, and without so much as mentioning the fact) the one position and rejecting the other. He assumes that there is no source of warrant or knowledge in addition to reason. This is not self-evident; millions, maybe billions of Christians and others reject it. Is it sensible, then, just to *assume* it, without so much as acknowledging this contrary opinion, without so much as a feeble gesture in the direction of argument or reason?

C. HBC more Inclusive?
John Collins recognizes that Troeltschian scholarship involves theological assumptions not nearly universally shared. He does not argue for the truth of these assumptions, but recommends them on a quite different basis. Criticizing Brevard Childs's proposal for a 'canonical' approach to Scripture scholarship,[60] he claims that the problem is that the former does not provide an *inclusive context* for the latter:

> If biblical theology is to retain a place in serious scholarship, it must be
> … conceived broadly enough to provide a context for debate between dif-
> ferent viewpoints. Otherwise it is likely to become a sectarian reservation,
> of interest only to those who hold certain confessional tenets that are not
> shared by the discipline at large. Childs's dogmatic conception of the canon
> provides no basis for advancing dialogue. In my opinion historical
> criticism still provides the most satisfactory framework for discussion.[61]

He adds that:

> One criterion for the adequacy of presuppositions is the degree to which
> they allow dialogue between differing viewpoints and accommodate
> new insights.… Perhaps the outstanding achievement of historical criti-
> cism in this century is that it has provided a framework within which
> scholars of different prejudices and commitments have been able to
> debate in a constructive manner (Ibid., p. 8).

So why should we prefer Troeltschian Scripture scholarship over tradi-tional Bible commentary? Because it offers a wider context, one in which people with conflicting theological opinions can all take part. We may be conservative Christians, theological liberals, or people with no theological views whatever: we can all take part in Troeltschian Scripture scholarship, provided we acquiesce in its fundamental assumptions. This is why it is to be preferred to the more traditional sort.

Now this would perhaps be a reason for practicing *Duhemian* Scripture scholarship, but of course Troeltschian Scripture scholarship is not Duhemian: the principles upon which it proceeds are not accepted by nearly everyone. They would be accepted by only a tiny minority of contemporary Christians, for example. And this shows a fundamental confusion, so it seems to me, in Collins's defence of Troeltschian scholarship. The defense he offers is appropriate for *Duhemian* scholarship; it is not at all appropriate for *Troeltschian* scholarship. The principles of Troeltschian historical scholarship, so interpreted as to preclude miracle, direct divine action, and special divine inspiration of the Bible, are extremely controversial philosophical and theological assumptions. Those who do not accept these controversial assumptions will not be inclined to take part in Troeltschian HBC, just as those who do not accept traditional Christian philosophical and theological views will not be likely to engage in traditional Biblical commentary. (If you do not think the Lord speaks in Scripture, you will be unlikely to spend a great deal of your time trying to figure out what it is God says there.) As John Levenson puts it, historical criticism "does not facilitate communication with those outside its boundaries: it requires fundamentalists, for example, to be born again as liberals—or to stay out of the conversation altogether." He adds that "if inclusiveness is to be gauged quantitatively, then [Brevard] Childs would win the match hands down, for far more people with biblical interests share Christian faith than a thoroughgoing historicism. Were we historical critics to be classed as a religious body we should have to be judged a most minuscule sect indeed —and one with a pronounced difficulty relating to groups that do not accept our beliefs."[62]

V. *Nothing to be Concerned* About

We are now prepared to return to Harvey's original question: why is it that the person in the pew pays little attention to the contemporary HBC, and, despite those decades of research, retains rather a traditional picture of the life and ministry of Jesus? As to why *in actual historical fact* this is the case, this is a job for an intellectual historian. What we have seen so far, however, is that there is no compelling or even reasonably decent argument for supposing that the procedures and assumptions of HBC are to be preferred to those of traditional Biblical commentary. A little epistemological reflection enables us to see something further: the traditional Christian (whether in the pew or not) has a good reason to reject the skeptical claims of HBC and continue to hold traditional Christian belief despite the allegedly corrosive acids of HBC.

A. Troeltschian HBC Again

As we have seen, there are substantially three types of HBC. For present purposes, however, we can consider Duhemian and Spinozistic HBC together.
Let us say, therefore, that we have both Troeltschian and non-Troeltschian
HBC. Consider the first. The Troeltschian Scripture scholar accepts Troeltsch's
principles for historical research, under an interpretation according to which
they rule out the occurrence of miracles and the divine inspiration of the
Bible (along with the corollary that the latter enjoys the sort of unity accruing
to a book that has one principal author). But then it is not at all surprising
that the Troeltschian tends to come up with conclusions wildly at variance
with those accepted by the traditional Christian. As Gilkey says, "Suddenly
a vast panoply of divine deeds and events recorded in scripture are no longer
regarded as having actually happened" (above, p. 255). Now if (instead of
tendentious claims about our inability to do otherwise) the Troeltschian
offered some good reasons to think that in fact these Troeltschian principles
are *true*, then the traditional Christian would certainly have to pay attention;
then she might be obliged to take the skeptical claims of historical critics
seriously. But Troeltschians apparently do not offer any such good reasons.
They simply declare that nowadays we cannot think in any other way, or
(following Harvey) that it is immoral to believe in, e.g., Christ's resurrection
on other than historical grounds.

Neither of these is remotely persuasive as a reason for modifying traditional Christian belief in the light of Troeltschian results. As for the first, of
course, the traditional Christian knows that it is quite false: she herself and
many of her friends nowadays (and hundreds of millions of others) do think
in precisely that proscribed way. And as far as the implicit claims for the
superiority of these Troeltschian ways of thinking go, she will not be impressed by them unless some decent arguments of one sort or another are
forthcoming, or some other good reason for adopting that opinion. The mere
claim that this is what many contemporary experts think will not and should
not intimidate her. And the second proposed reason (Harvey's reason) seems
to be itself dependent on the very claim at issue. Clearly the critic thinks it
immoral to form beliefs about historical facts on grounds other than historical research because he believes that the only reliable grounds for beliefs of
the former type is research of the latter type. Again, however, he offers no
argument for this assumption, merely announcing it as what those in the
know believe, and perhaps also adopting an air of injured puzzlement about
the fact that the person in the pew does not seem to pay much attention.

To see the point here, consider an analogy: suppose your friend is accused
and convicted of stealing an ancient and valuable Frisian vase from the local
museum. As it happens, you remember clearly that at the time this vase was
stolen, your friend was in your office defending his eccentric views about
the gospel of John. You have testified to this in court, but to no avail. I come
along and offer to do a scientific investigation to see whether your view here

is in fact correct. You are delighted, knowing as you think you do that your friend is innocent. When I explain my methods to you, however, your delight turns to dismay. For I refuse to accept the testimony of memory; I propose to ignore completely the fact that you *remember* your friend's being in your office. Further, my method precludes from the start the conclusion that your friend is innocent, even if he *is* innocent. Could I blame you for losing interest in my 'scientific' investigation? But the traditional Christian ought to view Troeltschian HBC with the same suspicion: it refuses to admit a source of warranted belief (the testimony of Scripture) the traditional Christian accepts, and is precluded in advance from coming to such conclusions as that Jesus really did arise from the dead and really is the divine Son of God.

B. Non-Troeltschian HBC

Troeltschian HBC, therefore, has no claim on a serious Christian; it is wholly reasonable for her to form and maintain her beliefs quite independently of it. How about non-Troeltschian (Duhemian and Spinozistic) HBC? This is, of course, a very different kettle of fish. The non-Troeltschian proposes to employ only assumptions that are clearly deliverances of reason (or accepted by everyone party to the project). She does not (for purposes of scholarship) accept the traditional Christian's views about the Bible or the life of Christ, but she also does not accept Troeltsch's principles. She does not assume that miracles did or could not happen; but of course that is quite different from assuming that they did not or could not, and she does not assume that either. She does not assume that the Bible is in fact a word from the Lord and hence authoritative and reliable; but she also does not assume that it is not.

Of course, that may not leave her a lot to go on. The non-Troeltschian is handicapped in this area in a way in which she is not in such areas as physics or chemistry. In the latter, there is little by way of theological controversy that seems relevant to the pursuit of the subject. Not so for Scripture scholarship; here the very foundations of the subject are deeply disputed. Does the Bible have one principal author, namely God himself? If not, then perhaps Jowett—"Scripture has one meaning—the meaning which it had to the mind of the prophet or evangelist who first uttered or wrote, to the hearers or readers who first received it"—is right; otherwise, he is wrong.[63] Is it divinely inspired, so that what it teaches is both true and to be accepted? If it reports miraculous happenings—risings from the dead, a virgin birth, the changing of water into wine, healings of people blind or lame from birth—are these to be taken more or less at face value, or dismissed as contrary to "what we now know"? Is there an entry into the truth about these matters—faith or divine testimony by way of Scripture, for example—quite different from ordinary historical investigation? If we prescind from all these matters and proceed responsibly (remembering to shun the Fallacy of Creeping Certitude, for example), what we come up with is likely to be pretty slender.

A. E. Harvey, for example, proposes the following as beyond reasonable doubt from everyone's point of view, i.e., Duhemianly: "that Jesus was known in both Galilee and Jerusalem, that he was a teacher, that he carried out cures of various illnesses, particularly demon-possession and that these were widely regarded as miraculous; that he was involved in controversy with fellow Jews over questions of the law of Moses: and that he was crucified in the governorship of Pontius Pilate."[64] It is not even clear whether Harvey means that the *conjunction* of these propositions is beyond reasonable doubt, or only each of the conjuncts;[65] in either case what we have is pretty slim.

Or consider John Meier's monumental *A Marginal Jew: Rethinking the Historical Jesus.*[66] Meier aims to be Duhemian, or anyway Spinozistic: "My method follows a simple rule: it prescinds from what Christian faith or later Church teaching says about Jesus, without either affirming or denying such claims" (Meier, *A Marginal Jew*, p. 1). (I think he also means to eschew assumptions incompatible with traditional Christian belief.) Meier's fantasy of "an unpapal conclave" of Jewish, Catholic, Protestant and agnostic scholars, locked in the basement of the Harvard Divinity School library until they come to consensus on what historical methods can show about the life and mission of Jesus, is thoroughly Duhemian. This conclave, he says, would yield "... a rough draft of what that will-o'-the-wisp 'all reasonable people' could say about the historical Jesus." (Ibid., p. 2). Meier sets out, judiciously, objectively, carefully, to establish that consensus.[67] What is striking about his conclusions, however, is how slender they are, and how tentative—and this despite the fact that on occasion he cannot himself resist building occasional towers of probability. About all that emerges from Meier's painstaking work is that Jesus was a prophet, a proclaimer of an eschatological message from God, someone who performs powerful deeds, signs and wonders, that announce God's kingdom, and also ratify his message.[68] As Duhemian or Spinozist, of course, we cannot add that these signs and miracles involve special or direct divine action; nor can we say that they do not. We cannot say that Jesus rose from the dead, or that he did not; we cannot conclude that Scripture is specially inspired, or that it is not.

Now what is characteristic of non-Troeltschian HBC is just that it does not involve those Troeltschian principles: but of course it also rejects any alleged source of warranted belief in addition to reason (Spinozistic) and any theological assumptions not shared by everyone party to the discussion. Traditional Christians, rightly or wrongly, think they do have sources of warranted belief in addition to reason: faith and the work of the Holy Spirit, or divine testimony in Scripture, or the testimony of the Spirit-led church. They may of course be *mistaken* about that; but until someone gives a decent argument for the conclusion that they *are* mistaken, they need not be impressed by the result of scholarship that ignores this further source of belief. If you want to learn the truth about a given area, you should not restrict yourself to only *some* of the sources of warranted belief (as does the Spinozist), or only to beliefs accepted by everyone else (with the Duhemian); maybe you know something some of the others do not. Perhaps you remember that your friend was in your office expostulating about the errors of postmodernism at the very time he is supposed to have been stealing that Frisian vase; if no one else was there, then you know something the rest do not.

So the traditional Christian need not be fazed by the fact that non-Troeltschian HBC does not support her views about what Jesus did and said. She thinks she knows some things by faith—that Jesus arose from the dead, for example. She may concede that if you leave out of account all that she knows in this way, then with respect to the remaining body of knowledge or belief the resurrection is not particularly probable. But that does not present her with an intellectual or spiritual crisis. We can imagine a renegade group of whimsical physicists proposing to reconstruct physics, refusing to use belief that comes from memory, say, or perhaps memory of anything more than one minute ago. Perhaps something could be done along these lines, but it would be a poor, paltry, truncated, trifling thing. And now suppose that, say, Newton's Laws or Special Relativity turned out to be dubious and unconfirmed from this point of view: that would presumably give little pause to the more traditional physicists. This truncated physics could hardly call into question physics of the fuller variety.

Similarly here. The traditional Christian thinks she knows *by faith* that Jesus was divine and that he rose from the dead. But then she will be unmoved by the fact that these truths are not especially probable on the evidence to which non-Troeltschian HBC limits itself. Why should that matter to her? So this is the rest of the answer to Harvey's question: if the HBC in question is non-Troeltschian, then the fact it does not verify traditional Christian beliefs is due to its limiting itself in the way it does, to its refusing to use all the data or evidence the Christian thinks he has in his possession. For a Christian to confine himself to the results of non-Troeltschian HBC would be a little like trying to mow your lawn with nail scissors or paint your house with a tooth-brush; it might be an interesting experiment if you have time on your hands, but otherwise why limit yourself in this way?

More generally, then: HBC is either Troeltschian or non-Troeltschian. If the former, then it begins from assumptions entailing that much of what the traditional Christian believes is false; but then it is no surprise that its conclusions are at odds with traditional belief. It is also of little direct interest to the traditional Christian. It offers her no reason at all for rejecting or modifying her beliefs; it also offers little promise of enabling her to achieve better or deeper insight into what actually happened. As for non-Troeltschian HBC, on the other hand, this variety of historical criticism omits a great deal of what she sees as relevant evidence and relevant considerations. It is therefore left with little to go on. But again, the fact that it fails to support traditional belief will be of little direct interest to the traditional believer; that is only to be expected, and casts no doubt at all upon that belief. Either way, therefore, the traditional Christian can rest easy with the claims of HBC; she need feel no obligation, intellectual or otherwise, to modify her beliefs in the light of its claims and alleged results.[69]

Concluding Coda

But is not all of this just a bit too sunny? Is not it a recipe for avoiding hard questions, for hanging onto belief no matter what, for guaranteeing that you will never have to face negative results, even if there *are* some? "HBC is either Troeltschian or non-Troeltschian: in the first case it proceeds from assumptions I reject; in the second it fails to take account of all of what I take to be the evidence; either way, therefore, I need not pay attention to it." Could not I say this *a priori*, without even examining the results of HBC? But then there must be something defective in the line of thought in question. Is not it clearly *possible* that historians should discover facts that put Christian belief into serious question, count heavily against it? Well, maybe so. How could this happen? As follows. HBC limits itself to the deliverances of reason; it is possible, at any rate in the broadly logical sense, that just by following ordinary historical reason, using the methods of historical investigation endorsed or enjoined by the deliverances of reason, someone should find powerful evidence against central elements of the Christian faith;[70] if this happened, Christians would face a genuine faith-reason clash. A series of letters could be discovered, letters circulated among Peter, James, John and Paul, in which the necessity for the hoax and the means of its perpetration are carefully and seriously discussed; these letters might direct workers to archeological sites in which still more material of the same sort is discovered.[71] The Christian faith is a *historical* faith, in the sense that it essentially depends upon what did in fact happen: "And if Christ has not been raised, your faith is futile" (I Cor. 15:17). It could certainly happen that by the exercise of reason we come up with powerful evidence[72] against something we take or took to be deliverance of the faith.[73] It is conceivable that the assured results of HBC should include such evidence. Then Christians would have a problem, a sort of conflict between faith and reason.

But, of course, nothing at all like this has emerged from HBC, whether Troeltschian or non-Troeltschian; indeed, there is little of any kind that can be considered its 'assured results', if only because of the wide-ranging disagreement among those who practice HBC.[74] We do not have anything like assured results (or even reasonably well-attested results) that conflict with traditional Christian belief in such a way that belief of that sort can continue to be accepted only at considerable cost; nothing like this has happened. What would be the appropriate response if it *did* happen, or rather if I came to be convinced that it had happened? Would I have to give up Christian faith, or else give up the life of the mind? What would be the appropriate response?

Well, what would be the appropriate response if I came to be convinced that someone had given a wholly rigorous, ineluctable disproof of the existence of God, perhaps something along the lines of J. N. Findlay's alleged ontological disproof?[75] Or what if, with David Hume (at least as understood by Thomas Reid), I come to think that my cognitive faculties are probably not reliable, and go on to note that I form this very belief on the basis of the very faculties whose reliability this belief impugns? If I did, what would or should I do—stop thinking about these things, immerse myself in practical activity (maybe playing a lot of backgammon, maybe volunteering to help build houses for Habitat for Humanity), commit intellectual suicide? I do not know the answer to any of these questions. There is no need to borrow trouble, however: we can think about crossing these bridges when (more likely, if) we come to them. [See 76, p. 278.]

NOTES

1   "New Testament Scholarship and Christian Belief" (hereafter 'NTS'), in *Jesus in History and Myth* (Buffalo, NY: Prometheus Books, 1986), p. 193.
2   I therefore concur (for the most part) both with C. Stephen Evans in his excellent *The Historical Christ and the Jesus of Faith: the Incarnational Narrative as History* (Oxford: Clarendon Press, 1996), and with Peter van Inwagen in "Critical Studies of the New Testament and the User of the New Testament", *God, Knowledge, and Mystery* (Ithaca, NY: Cornell University Press, 1995), pp. 163–190.
3   For an account of warrant, that property which distinguishes knowledge from mere true belief (a lucky guess, for example), see my *Warrant: The Current Debate* and *Warrant and Proper Function* (New York, NY: Oxford University Press, 1993).
4   See *Warrant and Proper Function*, pp. 34–35.
5   Nicholas Wolterstorff, *Divine Discourse: Philosophical Reflections on the Claim that God Speaks* (Cambridge: Cambridge University Press, 1995), p. 295.
6   More exactly, perhaps the probability of (1) on B is as high as .9, the probability of (2) on (1)&B as high as .9, and the same for P((3)/(B&(1)&(2))) and P((4)/(B&(1)&(2)&(3))). For more on this form of argument, see *Warranted Christian Belief*, chapter 8, "The Extended A/C Model: Revealed to our Minds."
7   Jonathan Edwards: "And the opening to view with such clearness, such a world of wonderful and glorious truth in the gospel, that before was unknown, being quite above the view of a natural eye, but appearing so clear and bright, has a powerful and invincible influence on the soul to persuade of the divinity of the gospel." *The Religious Affections* (New Haven, CT: Yale University Press, 1959), p. 303.
8   I do not for a moment mean to suggest that teaching us truths is *all* that the Lord intends in Scripture: there is also raising affection, teaching us how to praise, how to pray, how to see the depth of our own sin, how marvelous the gift of salvation is, and a thousand other things.
9   See, for example, Richard Swinburne (*Revelation* (Oxford: Clarendon Press, 1992), p. 192), who suggests that Paul's Christology at Romans 1:4 should be understood in terms of the 'high' Christology of the first chapter of John's gospel. We could say the same for Paul's Christology in his speech in Acts 13, where he seems to suggest that a special status was *conferred* on Jesus, as opposed to John 1, according to which Jesus is the incarnation of the preexistent Word. See also Raymond Brown, *New Testament Christology* (New York, NY: Paulist Press, 1994), pp. 133ff.
10   Of course this procedure, like most others, can be and has been abused; that possibility in itself, however, is nothing against it, though it should serve as a salutary caution.
11   A further complication: we cannot simply assume that there is some one thing, the same for everyone, that the Lord intends to teach in a given passage; perhaps what he intends to

teach me, or my relevant sociological group, is not the same as what he intended to teach a fifth century Christian.

12 *Tractatus theologico-politicus*, 14. Of course, this method does not preclude a rational argument (an argument from reason alone) for the proposition that indeed there has been a divine revelation, and that the Bible (or some part of it) is precisely that revelation: exactly this was John Locke's project.

13 To understand historical criticism and its dominance properly, says David Yeago, one must understand "the historic coupling of historical criticism with a 'project to the Enlightenment' aimed at liberating mind and heart from the shackles of ecclesiastical tradition. In the modern context, claims to 'Enlightenment' must be backed up with the claim to have achieved a proper *method*, capable of producing real knowledge to replace the pre-critical confusion and arbitrariness of tradition." "The New Testament and the Nicene Dogma", *Pro Ecclesia* Vol. III, No. 2 (Spring, 1994), p. 162.

14 *The Virginal Conception and Bodily Resurrection of Jesus* (New York, NY: Paulist Press, 1973), p. 6.

15 See also John P. Meier, *A Marginal Jew: Rethinking the Historical Jesus* (New York, NY: Doubleday, 1991, two volumes), p. 1.

16 Nor can you employ a proposition which is such that the warrant it has for you comes from some proposition you know or believe by faith; we might put this by saying that in doing science you cannot employ any proposition whose epistemic provenance, for you, includes a proposition you know or believe by faith.

But is this really true? Why should we believe it? What is the status of the claim that if what you are doing is science, then you cannot employ, in your work, any proposition you believe or know by faith? Is this supposed to be true by definition? If so, whose definition? Is there a good argument for it? Or what? See my "Methodological Naturalism?", *Facets of Faith and Science*, ed. J. van der Meer (Lanham, MD: University Press of America, 1996), pp. 177–222.

17 Thus Benjamin Jowett (the 19th century Master of Balliol College and eminent translator of Plato): "Scripture has one meaning—the meaning which it had to the mind of the prophet or evangelist who first uttered or wrote, to the hearers or readers who first received it." "On the Interpretation of Scripture", in *The Interpretation of Scripture and Other Essays* (London: George Routledge & Sons, 1906), p. 36. Quoted in Jon D. Levenson, *The Hebrew Bible, the Old Testament, and Historical Criticism* (Louisville, KY: Westminster/John Knox Press, 1993), p. 78. Jowett was not a paragon of intellectual modesty, which may explain a poem composed and circulated by undergraduates at Balliol:
First come I, my name is Jowett.
There's no knowledge but I know it.
I am the master of the college.
What I don't know isn't knowledge.

18 E. P. Sanders, *Jesus and Judaism* (Philadelphia, PA: Fortress Press, 1985), p. 5.

19 Levenson, p. 109.

20 "Jesus Risen: Bodily Resurrection But No Empty Tomb", *Theology* Vol. 89 No. 728 (March, 1986), p. 91.

21 *The Real Jesus: The Misguided Quest for the Historical Jesus and the Truth of the Traditional Gospels* (San Francisco, CA: HarperSanFrancisco, 1996), p. 172. The target of much of Johnson's criticism is the notorious 'Jesus Seminar'.

22 I do not mean to suggest, of course, that the traditional Biblical commentator cannot also investigate these questions; if she does, however, it will be in the ultimate service of an effort to discern what the Lord is teaching in the passages in question.

23 See especially his "Über historische und dogmatische Methode in der Theologie" in his *Gesammelte Schriften* (Tubingen: Mohr, 1913) Vol. 2, pp. 729–753, and his article "Historiography" in James Hastings (ed.). *Encyclopedia of Religion and Ethics* Vol. VI (Edinburgh: T & T Clark, 1925), pp. 716–723.

24 "Is Critical Biblical Theology Possible?" in *The Hebrew Bible and its Interpreters*, eds. William Henry Propp, Baruch Halpern and David Freedman (Winona Lake, IN: Eisenbrauns, 1990), p. 2.

25 Subtitled *The Morality of Historical Knowledge and Christian Belief* (New York, NY: Macmillan, 1966).

26 "Historiography", p. 718.

27 Thus Descartes (part 2 of *Principles of Philosophy*) in stating something like a law of conservation of momentum: xxvii. The first law of nature: that each thing as far as in it lies, continues always in the same state; and that which is once moved always continues so to move.

28 An opinion preserved among such contemporary philosophers as David Armstrong (see his *What is a Law of Nature?* (Cambridge: Cambridge University Press, 1984)) and David Lewis (see, e.g., his "New Work for a Theory of Universals", *Australasian Journal of Philosophy* Vol. 61 No. 4 (December 1983), pp. 343ff.).

29 See, in particular, Bas van Fraassen's *Laws and Symmetry* (Oxford: Clarendon Press, 1989) for an extended and powerful argument against the exercise of natural laws.

30 *Existence and Faith*, ed. Schubert Ogden (New York, NY: Meridian Books, 1960), pp. 291–292. Writing 50 years before Troeltsch, David Strauss concurs: "… all things are linked together by a chain of causes and effects, which suffers no interruption." *Life of Jesus Critically Examined* (Philadelphia, PA: Fortress Press, 1972), sec. 14. (Quoted in Harvey, *The Historian and the Believer*, p. 15.)

31 *Principles of Christian Theology*, 2nd ed. (New York: Charles Scribner's Sons, 1977), p. 248.

32 "Cosmology, Ontology and the Travail of Biblical Language", reprinted in Owen C. Thomas, ed., *God's Activity in the World: the Contemporary Problem* (Chico, CA: Scholars Press, 1983), p. 31.

33 "La Philosophie scientifique de M. Duhem", *Revue de Métaphysique et de Morale*, XII (July, 1904), pp. 699ff.

34 See the appendix to Duhem's *The Aim and Structure of Physical Theory*, trans. Philip P. Wiener, foreword by Prince Louis de Broglie (Princeton, NJ: Princeton University Press, 1954) (the book was first published in 1906). The appendix is entitled "Physics of a Believer" and is a reprint of Duhem's reply to Rey; it was originally in the *Annales de Philosophie chrétienne* Vol I (Oct. and Nov. 1905), pp. 44ff. and 133ff.

35 Of course, this proposal must be qualified, nuanced, sophisticated. It makes perfect sense for me to continue to work on a hypothesis after others have decided it is a dead end; science has often benefited from such disagreements.

36 To be sure, it may be difficult to specify the relevant community. Suppose I am a Scripture scholar at a denominational seminary: what is my relevant community? Scripture scholars of any sort, all over the world? Scripture scholars in my own denomination? In western academia? The people, academics or not, in my denomination? Christians generally? The first thing to see here is that our Scripture scholar clearly belongs to many different communities, and may accordingly be involved in several different scholarly projects.

37 *A Marginal Jew: Rethinking the Historical Jesus*, p. 1.

38 According to Spinoza, as we saw, "The rule for [Biblical] interpretation should be nothing but the natural light of reason …" (above p. 250).

39 The author of *The Life of Jesus, Critically Examined* (London: Sonnenschein, 1892), one of the earliest higher critical salvoes.

40 "Translator's Preface", *Calvin's Commentaries*, Vol. xvi, trans. the Rev. William Pringle (Grand Rapids, MI: Baker Book House, 1979), p. vi. Pringle's preface is dated at Auchterarder, Jan. 4, 1845.

41 John D. Levenson, "The Hebrew Bible, the Old Testament, and Historical Criticism" in *The Hebrew Bible, the Old Testament, and Historical Criticism*, p. 9. (An earlier version of this essay was published under the same title in *Hebrew Bible or Old Testament? Studying the Bible in Judaism and Christianity*, eds. John Collins and Roger Brooks (Notre Dame, IN: University of Notre Dame Press, 1990).) Of course, *clairvoyance* is not at issue at all: the question is really whether the Scripture has one principal author, namely God. If it does, then it does not require clairvoyance on the part of a human author for a passage from a given time to refer to something that happens much later. All that is required is God's omniscience.

42 *The New Testament as Canon: An Introduction* (Valley Forge, PA: Trinity Press International, 1984, 1994), p. xvii.

43 "The crisis grows out of the fact now freely admitted by both Protestant and Catholic theologians and exegetes: that as far as can be discerned from the available historical data, Jesus of Nazareth did not think he was divine [and] did not assert any of the messianic

claims that the New Testament attributes to him ..." Thomas Sheehan, *The First Coming*
(New York, NY: Random House, 1986), p. 9.
44 San Francisco: HarperSanFrancisco, 1992.
45 *Jesus the Magician* (New York, NY: Harper and Row, 1978).
46 *What Really Happened to Jesus: A Historical Approach to the Resurrection* (Louisville, KY:
Westminster/John Knox Press, 1995).
47 "The Historicity of Jesus" in *Jesus in History and Myth*, eds., R. Joseph Hoffman and Gerald
A. Larue (Buffalo, NY: Prometheus Books, 1986), pp. 27ff.
48 *The Sacred Mushroom and the Cross* (Garden City, NY: Doubleday and Co., 1970).
49 Sheehan, *op. cit.*
50 As we have just seen. This lack of accord is especially well documented by Stephen Evans
(op. cit.), pp. 322ff.
51 *Kerygma and Myth* (New York, NY: Harper and Row, 1961), p. 5. Compare Marcus Borg's
more recent comment: "... to a large extent, the defining characteristic of biblical scholarship
in the modern period is the attempt to understand Scripture without reference to another
world because in this period the visible world of space and time is the world we think of as
'real.'" ("Root Images and the Way We See", *Fragments of Infinity* (Dorset, UK, & Lindfield,
Australia, 1991), p. 38. Quoted in Huston Smith's "Doing Theology in the Global Village",
Religious Studies and Theology, Vol. 13/14, No. 2/3, (December, 1995), p. 12. On the other
side, note Abraham Kuyper (*To Be Near Unto God*, trans. John Hendrik de Vries (Grand
Rapids, MI: Wm. B. Eerdmans Publishing Co., 1918), pp. 50–51); writing not long after the
invention of the "wireless", he saw it not as an obstacle to traditional faith but as a sort
of electronic symbol of the way in which each of us can communicate instantaneously
with God.
52 We might call this the preemptive 'we': those who do not agree with us on the point in
question are (by comparison with us) so unenlightened that we can properly speak as if
they do not so much as exist.
53 Some, however, might see here little more than an effort to gain standing and respectability
in a largely secular academia by adopting a stance that is, so to say, more Catholic than the
Pope.
54 Here I can be brief; William Alston has already proposed a compelling argument for the
claim I propose to support, namely, that one can perfectly well do science even if one thinks
God has done and even sometimes still does miracles. See his "Divine Action: Shadow or
Substance?" in *The God Who Acts: Philosophical and Theological Explorations*, ed. Thomas F.
Tracy (University Park, PA: Penn State University Press, 1994), pp. 49–50.
55 As Alston argues.
56 I *think* the argument is intended to support Troeltschian HBC; it could also be used,
however, to support Spinozistic or (less plausibly) Duhemian HBC.
57 NTS, pp. 194ff.; a fuller (if older) and influential presentation of his views is to be found in
his *The Historian and the Believer*.
58 Described with insight and verve in James C. Livingston's monograph *The Ethics of Belief:
An Essay on the Victorian Religious Conscience* in the American Academy of Religion's *Studies
in Religion* (Tallahassee, FL, and Missoula, MT: Scholars Press, 1978). I thank Martin Cook
for calling my attention to this monograph.
59 First published in *The Contemporary Review* (XXIX, 1877); reprinted in Clifford's *Lectures and
Essays* (London: Macmillan, 1879), pp. 354ff.
60 See, e.g., Childs's *The New Testament as Canon: An Introduction* (Valley Forge, PA: Trinity
Press International, 1994), pp. 3–53.
61 "Is a Critical Biblical Theology Possible?" in *The Hebrew Bible and its Interpreters*, pp. 6–7.
Collins speaks here not of Troeltschian HBC but of HBC simpliciter; a couple of pages
earlier, however, he identifies HBC with Troeltschian HBC.
62 Levenson, p. 120.
63 see note 17 above.
64 *Jesus and the Constraints of History* (London and Philadelphia: Westminster Press, 1982), p. 6.
65 It could be that each of the conjuncts is beyond reasonable doubt but that their conjunction
is not. Suppose (just to choose arbitrarily a number) what is probable to degree .95 or higher
is beyond reasonable doubt. Then if each of the above is beyond reasonable doubt, their
conjunction might still be little more than twice as probable as its denial.

66 New York, NY: Doubleday, 1991, 1994. The first volume has 484 pages; the second has 1,055 pages; a third volume is currently expected.
67 "Meier's treatment, in short, is as solid and moderate and pious as Historical Jesus scholarship is ever likely to be. More important, Meier is a careful scholar. There is nothing hasty or slipshod in his analysis; he considers every opinion, weighs every option." Johnson, p. 128.
68 See Johnson, pp. 130–131.
69 *Alleged* results: because of the enormous controversy and disagreement among followers of HBC, it is very difficult to find anything one could sensibly call 'results' of this scholarship.
70 Or, less crucially, evidence against what appear to be the teaching of Scripture. For example, archeological evidence could undermine the traditional belief that there was such a city as Jericho.
71 See Bas van Fraassen, "Three-sided Scholarship: Comments on the Paper of John R. Donahue, S. J.", in *Hermes and Athena*, eds. Eleonore Stump and Thomas Flint (Notre Dame, IN: University of Notre Dame Press, 1993), p. 322. "Finish it [the depressing scenario] yourself, if you have the heart to do it", says van Fraassen.
72 Or *think* we come up with it; even if we are mistaken about the evidence in question, it could still precipitate this sort of problem for us.
73 See my "When Faith and Reason Clash: Evolution and the Bible" in *Christian Scholar's Review*, Vol. XXI No. 1 (September, 1991), pp. 9–15.
74 Thus Harold Attridge in "Calling Jesus Christ" in *Hermes and Athena*, p. 211.: "There remains enormous diversity among those who attempt to describe what Jesus really did, taught, and thought about himself. For some contemporary scholars he was a Hellenistic magician; for others, a Galilean charismatic or rabbi; for yet others, a prophetic reformer; for others, a sly teller of wry and engaging tales; for some he had grandiose ideas; for others he eschewed them. In general, the inquirer finds the Jesus that her historical method allows her to see. It is as true today as it was at the end of the liberal quest for the historical Jesus catalogued by Albert Schweitzer that we moderns tend to make Jesus in our own image and likeness." The Schweitzer reference is to his *Von Reimarus zu Wrede* (1906), translated by W. Montgomery under the title *The Quest of the Historical Jesus: A Critical Study of its Progress from Reimarus to Wrede* (New York, NY: Macmillan, 1956).
75 "Can God's Existence be Disproved?" *Mind* Vol. 57 No. 226 (April, 1948), pp. 176–183.
76 My thanks to Mike Bergmann, John Cooper, Kevin Corcoran, Ronald Feenstra, Marie Pannier, Neal Plantinga, Tapio Puolimatka, David Vanderlaan, James VanderKam, Calvin Van Reken, and Henry Zwaanstra. A longer version of this paper appears as chapter 12 of *Warranted Christian Belief* (New York, NY: Oxford University Press, forthcoming).

SCRIPTURE AS POPULAR TEXT

KATHRYN TANNER

In contemporary theology it is not unusual for Christian claims about the universal and permanent pertinence of Scripture to draw upon theories of literary value for support. The Bible, like a classic or canonical text of a literary tradition, is no time-bound artifact of merely historical interest. Instead, it evinces the power to speak to people in a truth-bearing and transformative way across differences of time and place. In traditional theological language, what is at issue here is the odd power of the Word that Scripture proclaims to be ever contemporary in its salvific effects; or, perhaps more precisely, what is at issue here is the odd power of scriptural testimony to the Word, as that is ensured by the Holy Spirit of Jesus Christ, to be ever present in the power of that Word and that Spirit, whatever the historical circumstances, however geographically or temporally distant from the original apostolic witnesses. As a complement to such theological claims or a substitute for the supernaturalistic tenor of them, contemporary theologians often appeal to literary theories that affirm and offer an explanation for sharp differences of value among forms of writing: in both religious and non-religious contexts, only certain sorts of texts have a universal and lasting, trans-historical importance.

At bottom, both the theological and literary claim of value can be understood functionally or operationally. What both theologians and literary theorists are pointing out is that some texts, in a vast sea of possible contenders, pass the tests of time and geographical displacement. Such texts are taken up and read with interest by many different people, even those quite distant in time and space from their authors and original audiences. This common starting point—literary value understood in an operational or functional sense—is complicated, however, by the fact that literary theorists offer a number of different explanations for it. This paper lays out some of these differences in explanation in the form of a series of very general types of

Kathryn Tanner
The Divinity School, University of Chicago, Chicago, IL 60637, USA

positions, with the aim of assessing their usefulness for theology. Affirming the postmodern, cultural-studies drift of these accounts of literary value, I suggest that, rather than draw an analogy with high-culture classics, it makes better theological sense to think of the Bible as something like a popular text. When properly qualified, thinking of the Bible in that way enables the general style of biblical writing and reading to be hooked up with what are, in my view, theologically compelling accounts of biblical authority and of the God-world relation. How God acts for us and the shape of the Bible as a popular text conform with one another.[1]

Timeless Texts

The oldest—one might say the classic—explanation of the universal and permanent pertinence of certain texts tends to efface the historical and cultural particularity of both text and audience. A text speaks to all times and places because of the eternal, timeless values of its contents, and because the text is enabled thereby to address the humanity of its audience per se, without regard for the differences of time and place, the cultural and historical specificities, that distinguish people. Adolf von Harnack makes these points in a modern dress for Scripture. To show the Gospels' permanent value and validity is "to show what the essential elements in the Gospel are, and these elements are 'timeless.' Not only are they so; but the man (sic) to whom the Gospel addresses itself is also 'timeless,' that is to say, it is the man (sic) who, in spite of all progress ... , never changes in his innermost constitution and in his fundamental relations with the external world." Elaborating the latter point, "The oftener I re-read ... the Gospels, the more do I find that [their] contemporary discords ... sink into the background. I entertain no doubt that the founder had his eye ... upon man who, fundamentally, always remains the same, whether he be in riches or in poverty, ... of strong mind or of weak. It is the consciousness of all these oppositions being ultimately beneath it, and its own place above them, that gives the Gospel its sovereignty; for in every man it looks to the point that is unaffected by all these differences."[2]

According to this first general explanation, a text and its message have enduring value only to the extent they are transcendent, a-historical entities, somehow in time and space without succumbing to their vicissitudes. There is therefore no history of such texts and their proper reception, in any sense of genuine change and novelty; only a history of deviant readings and of failures to give them their proper due.[3] One can explain the rejection or misinterpretation of classic texts with reference to the historically-conditioned particularities of the audiences at issue. But no similar explanation is possible for the text's classic status: it is the very salience of such particularities —their getting in the way, their clamoring for primary attention—that interrupts the creation and proper recognition of classic texts.

The relation of a text to its changing audiences is not a focal point in this explanation of literary value, since the changing character of the audience seems a primary impediment to a text's classic standing. The more closely a text is associated with any of those changing audiences the less it appears a candidate for universal permanence. The very point of the explanation is to keep the text from close association with the particularities of the historically transient contexts in which it is produced and received. If one cannot get behind those diverse particularities to the human universals that such a text addresses, it is hard to attribute universal permanence to it. The text must not be addressing those particularities but something universal underneath them. The relationship that the text bears to changing audiences does not figure centrally, then, in this explanation of universal permanence because such a relationship has to be assumed to be always the same.

It is the qualities *of* the text that matter in this explanation of literary value and not what happens *between* it and the contexts of its production or reception. Instead of being a relational matter, what accounts for a text's universal permanence is the text's own intrinsic characteristics. What makes the text of enduring significance is something *in* the text, an internal feature of it, to which the particularities of its varying audiences contribute nothing.

Immunizing the text from any possible fall into transience and provinciality by way of its reception by historically particular readers is an identification of those intrinsic qualities with wholeness, completion, closure, and unity. In the face of what is already replete, the reader's role is simply to affirm or reject. The text achieves a universal and permanent pertinence in virtue of its ability to propose ever again a single, already constituted meaning or message for the simple acceptance (or rejection) of differently situated persons.

Within this same basic understanding of universal permanence it is possible to admit that such texts are part of the order of time and history. They might, for example, be discussed in that vein as historically conditioned parts of the Western heritage. The claim of their universal permanence then forces a privileging of the order of time and history of which they are a part. A new dualism arises, a dualism not between the historical and non-historical portions of human experience but between historical times, one central, one peripheral. There is an aspect of world history with the essential perpetuity and universality to match that of its constitutive literature. In short, Virgil speaks to all times and places because the Roman empire does. What exists outside that empire's orbit is of no account at all; what refuses to see itself as an integrated part of it is merely provincial. When the church becomes the carrier of that empire into medieval times, it is easy to think of both the Bible and Virgil in these same terms.[4] The dualism of historical times that enables the Bible to be considered something like a classic text can then find expression as the difference between salvation and secular history.

Within this same basic understanding of universal permanence, it is also possible to recognize the text's accommodation to later periods. In that case, later readers are not to accommodate *themselves* to an enduring message which is to be the same now as it was then. Instead, the enduring message of such texts accommodates itself, at least superficially, to the changing tenor of the times, in virtue of its own containment of multiple levels of sense. The enduring value of such texts is still to be found *in* them as some complete, full whole. It is indeed in virtue of that already realized fecundity that the text is able to give itself, in different forms, to all comers, able to offer itself with a different shape or dress to differently situated readers. The internal features of the text that account for its universal permanence now lie, however, at some depth beyond what the text obviously seems to say, on any simple reading. As works of poetic genius, divinely inspired texts, or places where the universal reason or logos speaks, one expects these texts to contain a number of senses at different levels of profundity—e.g., the literal, mystical, anagogical, typological etc. senses of Christian exegesis—senses that require interpretive digging if they are to be uncovered.[5]

The theological appeal of this type of account of universal permanence—like a number of other such types of accounts it may indeed be at least partly a theological production—is the way the qualities of classic texts match the traditional attributes of divinity. On this account, the Bible would have an aseity and self-sufficiency, a timelessness, and majestic power to demand obedience that are something like God's own. These parallels bring along with them, however, their own theological problems. Besides the possibly problematic association of these particular qualities with divinity (something that will concern us later), this way of accounting for differences in literary value either over- or under-identifies historical textual productions with the divine. The Bible itself, rather than what it witnesses to, the Bible *qua* human historical artifact with its own intrinsic literary qualities, is in effect divinized in a way that conflicts with the usual Christian insistence on a difference between God and world. And everywhere else God seems simply absent (e.g., the devil merely plays in historically changing church teachings about the Bible) in a way that conflicts with common Christian claims for God's overarching influence and presence. In short, the difference between God and creatures is turned into an intra-historical difference, dividing some texts from others in virtue of their intrinsic properties.

These theological reservations dovetail with the reservations of modern historical consciousness. From that perspective, it is clear, first of all, that nothing in space and time can be exempted from historical conditioning in the way this account of literary value seems to assume. In particular, nothing that is genuinely historical, genuinely human, can be walled off in this way from influence. Second, it is impossible to strip away the historical particularities of a text or its audiences, so as to distill something simply universal that has escaped essential determination by what historically precedes it and by present circumstances. What claims a universal and permanent pertinence must therefore be historically particular, a historically conditioned product. The exceptional character claimed for classic texts by this type of account is thereby relativized—it becomes a matter of more or less—and the distinction between texts is leveled: if some texts differ from others in their ability to speak across differences of time and place, they generate that capacity out of characteristics they share with all other genuinely historical texts.

Timely Texts

A new type of account of universal permanence follows from this recognition of inescapable historicity. Classic texts are now not timeless but ever timely. Indeed, in this type of account, the historical character of these texts is not simply ruefully admitted, but very often celebrated as the key to their ability to cross divides of space and time. Thus, in Gadamerian versions of this type, classic texts arise out of a definite historical location and speak to historically-situated persons. The bridge between them is also of an historical sort. Such texts have a history of effects in which their various audiences participate for all their historical distance from them. Understanding of human historicity is, then, the very thing that enables an understanding of classic texts, an understanding of the way they work.

In general for this type of account, explanations of universal pertinence center on the ability of some texts to establish relations of pertinence with audiences in varying times and in different places; it is this very ability that constitutes a text's universal pertinence. These accounts therefore focus on the nature of the relationship established with a changing context of reception and the conditions of its possibility.

With this shift in focus from the text itself to the interface of text and audience comes a willingness to admit the productive contribution of the reader to the sense of the text. Something approximating passive reception is no longer the ideal. The message of the text may itself change with differences in the contexts of its reception without jeopardizing its status as a classic text. Indeed, it is just this sort of ability to change that guarantees that status. Something new can always be made of them. Classic texts have, then, no already constituted meaning, before which they demand obeisance from historically-passing audiences; instead, such meaning arises in ever new forms as a result of the interaction of texts with the multiple, changing contexts of their reception.

This relational account of universal permanence does not eschew entirely, however, explanation in terms of the text's own properties. There is something about classic texts that enables them to be constantly reinterpreted and reworked to suit the needs of particular times and places. It is not, in other words, an historical accident that only some texts achieve this status. These texts have certain qualities that set them off from others.

Two quite distinct versions of an account of a classic's timeliness arise in this way: the qualities that the one uses to explain the timeliness of classic texts are denied by the other.

a) The Timeliness of Inexhaustible Meaning

In the first version, the identification of those properties approximates a great deal of the earlier account of classic timelessness that it replaces—and this is the source, in great part, of the second version's objections to it. The mix of Gadamerian and Ricoeurian hermeneutical themes in the work of David Tracy is a good case in point. Classic texts still appear to have some sort of inexhaustible fullness of content that accounts for their ability to speak across differences of time and place. They contain a surplus of meaning, in the sense of some semantic 'depth dimension' internal to the text itself. Despite the contributions of the reader, these texts seem constituted as already realized wholes directing the origination of new senses in ways appropriate for the particular context at issue. Emphasized thereby is the way in which the reader has first to submit herself to the text in order for the active (and perhaps ultimately critical) work of interpretation to proceed apace. Talk of the span of effective history that bridges text and reader serves the same function of dispelling the idea of control on the part of the human subject, who might otherwise confront the text as a mere object for interpretative manipulation: the reader is already a part of what she is to come to understand anew. So does the idea of split or double reference in literary (especially poetic or symbolic) expression: the reader is brought up short—surprised into stunned attention—by a world of meaning beyond any semiotic or semantic surface of a text that a reader could treat as a distanced and controllable object of ordinary apprehension.

One might argue, then, that this version of classic texts' timeliness is an historically-selfconscious updating of the older accommodation theory: the text is somehow still in control of its reception by way of its own internal amplitude, although now that control means no simple conformity, but a context-appropriate apprehension of the text's meaning that becomes thereby ever new. Texts are classic in virtue of an excessive fullness, which can never be exhausted or finally comprehended by any definitive act of interpretation. Their undrainable meaning is poured out in a never-ending historical stream of effects that conform to the particularities of the new terrain being covered—its questions and problems.

Moreover, like what we saw in the account of a classic's time*less*ness, both the meanings generated by classic texts and their readers are discussed in terms of human universals. Generalizations about the essentially human prevent the admission that classic texts are historically conditioned from suggesting that those texts are historically circumscribed as well, limited in their appeal, that is, to a particular historical community of readers. Classic texts of the Christian West, for example, must not be classic texts only for the

Christian West. To prevent that possibility, texts are said to attain the status of classics insofar as they disclose a possibility for being in the world that touches on something essentially human, something that is therefore a subject for recognition by the human in us all. The classics that are not religious disclose some aspect of what it means to be human—presumably that aspect that is salient at the time of their production—whereas religious classics capture the whole of what it means to be human under the grace of God, in a comprehensive or universal fashion. The classics produced by "artists, heroes, saints, and thinkers", allow "some recognition of an essential aspect of our existence—its fatedness, its challenge, its finitude, its horrors, its possibility, its joy", but "the *differentia* of the religious classic can be described as some 'self-manifestation (and concealment) of the whole by the power of the whole.'"[6] Simply put, the commonality of the issues raised by classic texts accounts for their universal interest. Classic texts, in order to be such, must disclose "a meaning and truth available in principle to all human beings."[7] And the same holds for religious classics; their distinctiveness merely makes the point more emphatically: "Any human being can interpret the religious classics because any human being can ask the fundamental questions that are part of the very attempt to become human at all, those questions that the religious classics address."[8]

Finally, despite the interpretation of classics in terms of reader response, what fundamentally explains a text's capacity to function as a classic is, as it was in the older theory of classic timelessness, something internal to the text. It is in virtue of its own internal qualities that a text contains or projects in front of it "a realized experience of that which is essential, that which endures."[9] The author has an experience of that sort; such an experience is then expressed in and through the linguistic workings of texts. It is those discursive features of texts—e.g., features of genre and style—that enable the original experience to be conveyed publicly to others and thereby freed from restriction to the author and her historical context. Such discursive features therefore seem to produce or disclose the meaning that is to be received differently by varying audiences in a relatively self-contained fashion, by way of their own internal capacities (e.g., the capacity for double reference found in poetic language). It is true that such discursive features work to engage the reader in a manner that respects her own imaginative capacities; it is also true that, in the case of religious classics, they are never adequate to the original experience. But the discursive features of classic texts nevertheless seem to bear meaning within them, as if they were a container or conveyer of it; or, if that is too strong, they at least work to produce or project it by way of discursive mechanisms, like double reference, that do not seem to require the contribution of the reader for their essential operation.

The theological appeal of this account of classic texts should be obvious; again, one might argue that it is in fact a secular generalization of Christian claims about the Bible.[10] The surprising, event-like character of the reader's

encounter with the classic text, for example, clearly suggests a general analogue for revelation by way of Christian Scripture, and replaces the more
message-like, propositional content for biblical revelation according to the
earlier account of the classic as timeless. When employed to understand
the universal pertinence of the Bible, this account of literary value also suggests the clear subordination of humans before a God who nevertheless
grants them a freedom of critical response.[11] We are always already God's
people in much the same way as we are always already people influenced
by this classic text; we are never in sovereign control of this text as we are
never in control of God. And yet God, through the classic of Scripture,
allows us to make sense for ourselves in a way that is genuinely novel in
keeping with the needs and interests of our ever-varying situations.

b) The Timeliness of Indeterminacy

The second version of an account of classic texts as timely explains that
timeliness by what the text lacks. Texts that speak to every time and place
are able to do so because of their indeterminacies, irreconciled pluralities,
their ambiguities, and absences. They are able to speak to every age because
they are capacious in their empty places, because they have room enough,
gaps aplenty, for all to position themselves within them. They are of con-
tinual interest because they always leave their audience with something to
do; readers are left with the task of understanding, a desire for sense that the
text holds out hope for but refuses in any direct way to appease. In short,
such texts are always reaching out to new readers by their failure to give a
definitive account of themselves.[12]

Such texts therefore call for the reader's active collaboration with them in
the construction of sense in a stronger way than was the case in the account
of timeliness as a function of plenitude. The reader's part or role is already
written into the classic's textual structure.[13] The reader does not merely re-
fashion a given structure or form, complete in itself, according to context and
her particular aesthetic sensibilities, to produce meaning. Instead, the structure of the text itself remains unfinished without the reader's active participa-
tion; its organization exists only as a field of possibilities or a set of tools for
construction, actively demanding the reader's entrance.[14] Rather than being
faced, so to speak, with an already completed score to be played in keeping
with the times and one's particular aesthetic sensibilities, one finds only a
series of possible permutations among which one must choose if there is to
be any playable score at all.[15]

Because of this open structure, the line between text and reader is blurred
in a way it was not before; in great part the reader is continuing the text
by her own linguistic operations. That would seem to mean, then, no awe-
inspired respect here for what precedes and disturbs the subject's desires for
control and autonomy. Yet, the classic text remains a constant challenge to
the reader's demand for simple sense. Indeed, the text remains a classic just

to the extent the linguistic extensions of the text by the reader—the reader's own commentary or interpretation of it—do not succeed in closing it off but leave its pluriform complexities available for fresh readings, in tension with its own. The text therefore has its own excessiveness; it ever exceeds its readers. It does so, however, by way of a surplus of signifiers, a complex discursive disorder, one might say, rather than by way of a surplus of inexhaustible meaning, already present in the form of some sort of unitary textual whole.

The primary opponent of such a view on the English-speaking scene is New Criticism, which takes to an extreme the kind of internalism and sense of textual completeness that one finds in the Gadamerian/Ricoeurian account to a lesser degree. New Critics emphasize the irony, paradox, and rich complexity of classic texts, but those qualities are thought to seal off such texts within their own self-enclosed realm of interlocking meaning and structure.[16] These are the features of a uniquely endowed poetic discourse which constructs its own world of sense, one inaccessible by way of the prose commentaries offered by its readers. No paraphrase is possible. The classic text should not *mean* but *be* in the sense that whatever meaning it has is inextricable from the organic character of its own literary structure. A close reading that follows the twists and turns of that structure is the only interpretation possible. Irony, paradox, and ambiguity do not serve to produce a text of lacunae. Instead, there is a many-leveled comprehensiveness to such poetic figures which demonstrates the text's unwillingness to see things by parts, as the active interests of a utilitarian consciousness might encourage. By way of such figures, the text sees all around the real complexities of life that rational discussion always obscures; it provides a total view. Moreover, the operations of those figures, like the worlds of meaning they construct, seem not to be subject to historical conditioning; their operations seem eternal and ahistorical. Classic texts become timeless wholes, verbal icons, independent and isolated from the historical worlds of their authors and readers.

The previous version of classic timeliness in terms of inexhaustible meaning obviously does not share New Criticism's view of the timeless character of classic texts and their sovereign autonomy vis-à-vis readers (whose contributions seem restricted therefore to the merely reiterative ones of attending to the formal structures of texts). But it does share with it the close association of poetic figures with claims to religious truth.[17] There is a kind of mystery to great works of literature that is akin to a religious one, a mysterious depth that prevents the reflective efforts of readers from ever rivaling the classic texts they interpret, thereby ensuring an unending interest in them. In both cases, texts generate their own world through their linguistic features, a whole of significance—whether they render or disclose it or whether that world is found in or before the text makes little difference here. Most fundamentally, both share the fundamental assumption of modernist literary theory: classic texts are complex wholes that for all their intricacy and multiplicity of levels hang together as a unity.[18] Texts are classic, they have a literary value that sets them off from others, in virtue of their complex unity.

It is this assumption of unity that comes under direct attack in the second version of classic timeliness. Unity is the reader's contribution, a demand the reader makes to texts which in and of themselves are constantly working to disturb it. Value is now put on texts with the ability to unsettle the expectation that everything will hang together in a unified way, texts with the potential to shake up every settled code of reading that readers bring to them.

This second version of classic texts' timeliness is of special interest to students of the Bible, since, especially to the theologically untrained eye, biblical texts seem to have the features mentioned. Unlike works of Greek literature or those of modern realistic novels, biblical stories seem full of holes; they are, as Erich Auerbach says, heavy with unexpressed background.[19] In the Bible, very little is said about where people have come from or what happens to them after the events of particular interest being related. Little direct description of scenes of action or personal characteristics is offered. Rather than confirm expectations of continuity and coherence of sense, these texts seem unwilling to iron out contradictions and tensions in the sources they employ. Later texts echo earlier ones in a way that does little to disguise the differences that remain between them: earlier texts are revised by later ones but continue to be heard in their earlier force. Multiple, irreconcilable versions of the same happenings are told. Stories are recounted in a kind of segmental way without any great effort to make explicit the narrative transitions or connections that bridge them.

Proponents of the first version of classic timeliness try simply to incorporate this apprehension of the Bible's pluriform "gapiness" within their own position; it is merely a salutary complication for this version's usual account of the construction of sense.[20] Tracy also shows he recognizes that the Bible has the features emphasized by the second version of timeliness when he admits that Scripture does not conform to the usual (modernist) expectations concerning an aesthetic masterpiece; the usual literary figures and techniques appear here in a broken form befitting the awful majesty of their subject matter.[21] He resists, however, making this very refusal of aesthetic harmony and order a key to the character of the classic.

Theologians like Hans Frei, who feel an affinity with New Criticism, react to its criticism in a similar fashion. Stung more sharply by such criticism, they relinquish the insistence on textual self-sufficiency and reader passivity characteristic of New Criticism, while resisting, to a perhaps much greater degree than Tracy, any relinquishing of unitary sense.[22] The text still produces its own world, the one world of the Bible, even if now in league with a community of readers who insist on reading it in a particular way.[23] If the text itself will not produce any particular world of meaning because of its own internal opacities and tensions, the reading community will, through norms for reading that effectively override impediments posed by the text. As William Placher points out in a recent essay, the tensions found in the different New Testament stories about Jesus need not present any problem when reading them as an identity description of Jesus: the same character can be rendered by them in any case.[24]

One might easily argue that none of these responses does full justice to the amount of disparity and disorder characteristic of the texts—e.g., is it all that clear that these different stories render the same character? But one could also simply argue, as I do now, that there are good theological reasons to pay more serious attention to the features of texts highlighted in the second version of classic timeliness. The theological benefits are of the sort that Robert Alter pointed to in his account of the prose portions of the Hebrew Bible.[25]

First of all, such texts set up a tension between the reader's expectation of narrative coherence and the fact of confusion on the surface level of the text that mirrors the theological idea of a difference between God's plan for the world and its realization in the messy affairs of human history. The author of the text—and ultimately God—knows the meaning of all that is told and how it all hangs together consistently, but this authorial authority is never directly revealed in what is said: the author does not directly state what the author knows. The text is full of "speaking silences" in the sense that it suggests the withholding of relevant information.[26] Rather than show its hand, in this text "character is revealed primarily through speech, action, and gesture, with all the ambiguities that entails; motive is frequently ... left in a penumbra of doubt; often we are able to draw plausible inferences about the personages and their destinies, but much remains a matter of conjecture or even of teasing multiple possibilities" (Alter, 158). Indeed, it seems that what the author relates—the messy affairs of human history—is not a suitable medium for such direct demonstration of the divine plan. God is at work in history but it is not obvious how what happens there is a fulfillment of divine intention. In between God's will and its realization in history come human beings with their ignorance of God's ways and their moral failings. The persons that these texts discuss seem free beings, for better or worse, persons who therefore can never simply mirror in their actions any divine plan that would take the form of an eternal, inexorably unrolling fate.

There is a divinely-given meaning to history but it is one that does not simply override the fact that human history is "a labyrinth of antagonisms, reversals, deceptions, shady dealings, outright lies, disguises, misleading appearances, and ambiguous portents."[27] This meaning to history is therefore not directly summarized by the texts, but indirectly *shown* in and through the narration of events. In keeping with the irregularity and confusion of ordinary life, those narrated events, moreover, display nothing of that unity of narrative continuity that a modernist reader would expect from a well-formed fiction or historical recounting. Continuity is suggested only through oddly recurring patterns of events and the revised repetition of words and phrases that are their analogue on the level of linguistic form. Thus, the parting of the Red Sea suggests the division of the waters in Genesis; or, the future of Israelite history repeats in a strange new form the pattern of events in the lives of the first husband and wife of the covenant with Abraham—betrothal, trial in the wilderness, blessing. No directly-stated, general meaning to history—even the sense that God is a gracious God—is used here to set up expectations in the reader that subsequent events of the narration will simply confirm. These narratives are not driven, as a modernist novel is, by the need to resolve a problem; they do not move from crisis to expected denouement. They are not texts that establish appropriate answers to come through the shape of prior questions asked. They are not texts that convey the realistic character of their narration by an appearance of inevitability in the way that what comes next—say, the next speech of a heroine—seems so fully in keeping with what came before—say, a fully rendered account of her motives and interests. Instead, what comes next is simply not predictable—that is the distinctive ambiguity of typological connections between events. Types are ambiguous and indistinct in their implications. Especially, when read in terms of New Testament intra-biblical exegesis, typological connections are as likely to include surprising reversals as simple continuities. Thus, in a very odd retelling of (among others) stories that concern how the second-born becomes first (e.g., Jacob and Esau), God's people are said to refuse the one, Jesus, who engrafts those without rights into the people of the covenant. No one could have expected this; and, despite the repetition of a biblical pattern, it is not at all obvious how the story remains the same one—the same tale of a God faithful to the people of Israel. In the search for a continuity of telling, one must not (so Paul affirms in Romans 9–11) rule out a surprising reversal of apparent privilege to come: Christians are susceptible to the same judgment and God's faithfulness to the Jews will somehow be confirmed in a new, improbable twist to the continuing tale.[28]

Popular Texts

If these are its theological virtues—a textual analogue to the mysteriousness of an uncontrollable God who can work with and need not override the messy features of human history that seem so different from God's own qualities—one major theological deficit in the account of timely indeterminacy is its association of classics with literary masterworks: the Bible is like James Joyce's *Ulysses*. The same tendency is characteristic of all the other accounts of the classic so far discussed.[29] They thereby miss the theological significance of the fact that, as Erich Auerbach pointed out many years ago, the Bible is not a typical high-culture work of literary artistry but something more like a popular text.[30] That was, indeed, the source of Greco-Roman repudiations of it: the Bible seems crude and inelegant, full of colloquial expressions and preoccupied with matters of poor taste. How ironic, then, that accounts of the Bible's textual privilege should avail themselves of theories that presume, in similar fashion to the Bible's ancient critics, a sharp difference in the literary value of texts. As Augustine averred, the Bible is not a difficult text but one whose style makes it accessible to all: "Those clear truths it contains it speaks without subterfuge, like an old friend, to the hearts of learned and unlearned alike. But even the truths which it hides in mysteries are not couched in such lofty style that a slow, uncultivated mind would not dare to approach them, as a poor man does not approach a rich one."[31] And the Bible treats with utmost seriousness even the most apparently mundane and trivial events of life, for everything can be of relevance to one's salvation, helping or hindering it. Everyone, no matter how humble of station, can therefore see the events of their own lives reflected in it. Contradicting the usual Greco-Roman association of style levels with types of subject matter, the Bible must find the humble worthy of serious treatment, since what is more important for salvation as Christians understand it than this humble one, Jesus, born in a manger and befriending the outcast? The unconditional character and universal scope of God's working in history—its gracious nature and radical inclusiveness—are matched in this way by the literary features of the Bible as a popular text.

Popularity, and the conditions for it, present, indeed, a new way of accounting for the classic character of texts. If one discounts the common associations of popularity with the ephemeral (i.e., the sense that what is popular today is unlikely to be tomorrow), then popularity becomes simply another way of discussing the functional or operational definition of the classic which all accounts of the classic use as their starting point: a classic text is a popular one in the sense that it seems able to speak to everyone, whatever their circumstances.

Accounts of popular texts, especially in recent cultural studies, tend to share a great deal with the account of timely indeterminacy; the account of classics as popular texts can therefore build on the latter's theological advantages. Both appeal basically to the same textual features in explaining reader interest: such texts are full of gaps. Using the Bible as the case in point, one could say, for example, that its refusal of detailed description is like that found in television situation comedies where no narrator voice-over provides any comprehensive overview and viewers are left to infer a depth of motivation and feelings from nothing more than a character's raised eyebrows, or tone of voice; fan gossip like biblical commentary fills in what is missing.[32] The parallel processing of information and associational logic necessary to understand the puns that so often grace trashy tabloid headlines are something like what reading the multiple versions of biblical tales requires.[33] The incoherent appearance of a New Testament canon that contains conflicting theological perspectives on Jesus' person is something like the tension-filled self-presentation of a Madonna who somehow manages to incorporate at once both a sexist view of women like her and a skepticism about the same tendencies of men to objectify the female form.[34]

This sort of overlap between the account of popular texts and the account of timely indeterminacy is no accident, since contemporary theories of popular texts are generally derived from the latter. Once the unity of classic texts becomes a function of reader response, the usual sharp divide between classic texts and others becomes a relative matter. A single set of categories can be used to discuss all texts, whether commonly identified as masterpieces or not. Literary theory becomes cultural studies, where Marvel Comics and *Finnegan's Wake* are first considered together before any judgments of value are proffered.[35]

The differences that remain between these two accounts can be brought out nicely by John Fiske's distinction between writerly and producerly texts, a distinction he spins out of Roland Barthes' talk of writerly and readerly texts in *S/Z*.[36] First, unlike writerly texts such as avant-garde novels which are the classics of timely indeterminacy, the producerly texts of popular culture do not force their readers into an active process of meaning production. They do not appear to be difficult texts; but rather seem to be talking about everyday reality in a down-to-earth way. They encourage everyone simply to take them up and read, without any worry about special training and without self-conciousness about the codes of reading brought to them. The Bible seems a text like this, encouraging the Christian habit of simply opening it at random with the expectation of finding something that will speak clearly to one's particular circumstance. Second, unlike writerly texts, when the difficulties in them are noticed (incoherences, ambiguities, and absences), these texts do not work of themselves to construct new rules for reading that must be accepted in order to make sense of them. These texts do not teach a new way of reading like avant-garde novels whose difficulty seems designed to point out, and therefore free the reader from, the usual literary conventions. They do not impose a new discipline, because, in keeping with what the first point of contrast implied, there are no formal prerequisites for making sense of them. Third, the interest in these texts is far more than literary. Their audience is not limited to an educated public, as the audience for avant-garde novels is—and this wider audience is interested in them, not for what they say about the literary conventions of reading, but for what they say about their lives. The relevance of these texts is social, one might say, rather than merely literary; one is tempted by them to read the details of one's everyday circumstances into them. Finally, insofar as these texts and everyday life are brought into contact in this way, the aesthetic distance which usually holds literary texts at arms length from everyday life is overcome. Text and life are blurred. One continues the text not only by extending the text in a new, similarly elite literary production—say, in a clever critical commentary published by a university press—but through the course of one's life. For example, in a kind of creative extension of her popular presentations (let us say these popular presentations are literally textual for the sake of easy comparison, taking the form perhaps of unauthorized biographies), one tries to become a girl like Madonna, writing fan letters, dressing strangely, attending concerts, discussing her new music videos on the phone with friends.

If the Bible is a popular text like this, we seem to see there a God of democratic power, patient persuasion, and far-reaching influence. The grace that comes to us through the Bible has no conditions placed on it. The text has the capacity to speak to us in the most mundane of circumstances, as in the highest. And whatever we get out of this text has certainly not been forced on us. Indeed, so much is this the case that the Bible seems unwilling to get us to see what it is trying to convey by any means that would ensure against failures of attention or shallow readings. The text does not demand attention to some privileged message within its pluriform complexity, nor does it always make any obvious claim on us, in a Gadamerian sense of *Anspruch*. Like the unclarity of typological connections within the history it narrates, the text does not supply any rule by which one could predict the future readings of it that are proper.

The major theological problem with this account of the classic as popular text, is that it seems to magnify a problem of textual authority to which the account of timely indeterminacy was also prone. (I reserved the problem for discussion now, because it appears here at its most extreme.) Like the latter account, an account of the classic in terms of popularity suggests that such texts depend in a strong sense on their readers for any production of a definite sense. Like the earlier account too, no sharp distinction is drawn between such texts and the discursive productions of their readers; those productions seem a continuation of the text at a similar level of value. All this might seem problem enough for theological affirmations of the authority of the Bible. In addition, however, and in contrast to the account of timely indeterminacy, the classic text now does not shatter the reading habits of its audience as a condition for making sense of it. Popular texts, as we have said, do not insist that they be read on their own terms; they do not establish terms. Authority in the form of critical purchase over its readers seems thereby threatened. Furthermore, popular texts seem not to have the authority to direct how they are received. As we mentioned, popular texts give no clear directions about how to read them, say, in the form of some new avant-garde code for reading without the expectation of beginning, middle, and end. Even more seriously, it is commonly said that popular reception resists or escapes the suggestions for reading made by the texts it enjoys; texts are only popular to the extent they may be subverted, even manipulated, by their audiences in line with their own ends. In particular, popular reading is said to be a reading against the grain of texts offered for mass consumption. For example, a television show is popular among working class people if it allows them to put those aspects of the show that resonate with their own

lives ahead of the preferred meanings of working class lives that its elite pro-
ducers intend to convey by means of the show—e.g., that working class people
are content for all their troubles. This work of reversal on the audience's part
explains in great part what makes the show a pleasurable experience for
them.

It may be, then, that the Bible has an exceptional authority for a popular
text, and that the account of popular texts should be modified accordingly in
theological use, so as to make sense of the unusual respect that Christians
believe this text is due. Indeed, none of the accounts of the classic that we
have discussed are sacrosanct. I follow Frei here in my willingness in principle to modify any general theory of literary value in order to do justice to
the oddities of this particular text (or, indeed, to do justice to oddities in the
appreciation of any text, whether biblical or not). But I believe the account of
popular texts is helpful as it stands for rethinking the notion of biblical
authority that theologians employ. It promotes a deeper investigation into
the nature of respect and disrespect.

It is true that popular reading gives no special respect to the text *qua* isolated object of value, as if it were some aesthetic object embodying universal
values of truth and beauty that raised it above the messy, transient particularities of everyday life. The account of timely indeterminacy still seems to
hold onto this idea of aesthetic distance, as do all the other theories of literary value that fail to question a sharp difference between high and low texts
at their root.[37] The respect that readers give to popular texts is respect of a
different sort, a respect that comes from expecting texts to be of everyday
relevance, to be useful for life.

It is true, secondly, that audience use of popular texts tends to be repet-
itive, almost reproductive, and often imitative, in a way that seems to show
an unwillingness to admit texts as finished artifacts and that seems to bridge
any sharp difference between texts and their audiences. Thus, popular readers
seem rarely satisfied with texts that are single and unrepeatable. They like
the text replayed whenever possible, in varying venues, from different angles;
and serialization is a popular pleasure. But is this failure ever to get enough
or failure to find satisfaction in the complete and the finished, any more a
form of disrespect than the repetition and serialization typical of Bible
reading in church? The true fan, moreover, blurs her own person with that
of her idol, but it would be hard to argue that this practice does not feed off
a perception of a sharp difference in value between a life lived with or
without such a personal identification. Is there not a comparable avoidance of
obvious deference in the *imitatio Christi*?

In the third place, it cannot be fair to say that popular readers do not
respect the direction of classic texts if the texts themselves do not offer that
direction. Underlying the theological complaint of disrespectful reading
may be, then, the counterfactual image of a biblical text that works to enforce
a unitary meaning, a text that offers a ready-made reading. One can only

properly respect the biblical text by respecting it for what it is—a text that is not anything like that image.

In the fourth place, while popular texts do not shatter the expectations of their audience as a condition for their making sense, they may very well shatter those expectations in the course of the reading. A parable is easy to understand in that one's literary competence is not at issue and the subject matter would seem quite run-of-the-mill, but that does not mean that the parable confirms our everyday expectations of the way the world works. Prodigal sons are not often welcomed home. Employees are not often paid as much as the hardest worker for doing next to nothing. No one invites just anyone off the street to their under-attended dinner parties. These stories resonate with one's everyday experience of family tensions, employment and fellowship around a table, because those everyday experiences are heard in and through the stories that overturn how things usually turn out—in acts of exclusion, conventional rigidity, and near-sightedness.

Fifth, popular reading typically only subverts and manipulates the texts it enjoys when such texts are designed by elites to reinforce dominant, conventional understandings of everyday life. Popular reading does not disrespect in the same fashion or degree texts that are themselves disrespectful of dominant conventions and established codes. Surely being addicted to the nightly news requires a greater effort of reading against the grain if you are a poor black youth living in the projects (the perennial subject of TV crime reports in my city of Chicago) than does being a fan of the rapper Queen Latifah's performance in the sentimental, 'rage against the machine' movie "Set It Off". Biblical parables, to use this example again, are of the latter general sort. They include the usual conventions and their warping in a way that either subordinates the former to the latter or makes their relationship unclear. It is no longer clear that the former, as in ordinary life, is the frame establishing the latter's deviance. It may in fact be the other way around: the usual conventions are shown to be deviant by setting them against the standards of, say, unmerited generosity and inclusive table fellowship.

Finally, while readers' expectations are not directly attacked by the popular text but given free rein at first, the plurality of possible readings always stands ready to contest the adequacy of any one. The only disrespectful reading from this point of view would be the reading that rules out alternative readings by disqualifying aspects of the texts that might give rise to them, by winnowing down what is important in the texts to only those portions that support a single privileged pattern of interpretation. In short, in order to respect the power of the text to contest the adequacy of one's own reading, one must not "excommunicate from the text the material that one does not employ."[38]

Perhaps one job of the theologian is to keep the biblical imagination open in this way, by offering not a new reading for a new time but a science of the possible, a sketch of what it is about this text that invites the unending production of multiple, quite disparate interpretations.[39] Rather than provide one's own singular exposition of the meaning of the Bible for today, or work to certify any particular Christian reading of it from past or present, the theologian's primary task, instead, would be to unsettle every Christian reading with reference to the possibilities that the Bible holds out for others, with reference to a biblical imagination wider than any extant church teaching.[40] The theologian's task would be to destabilize Christian accounts of the Bible, to put them in motion. Particularly worrisome would be those Christian readings of the Bible with the power and/or demonstrated tendency to dissolve the Bible into themselves, thereby cutting off their possible contestation by other interpreters (for instance, fundamentalist readings, the biblical interpretations favored by religious elites, or just Christian readings common in the present because so seemingly suitable to contemporary needs and attitudes).[41] By helping to put the Bible at a distance from the church, theology, in this form of a science of the possible, might promote a notion of biblical authority that is primarily proved, not by the Christian hope of taking clear direction from it, but by the Bible's ability to disturb Christian self-satisfaction and complacency.

NOTES

1 For a model of this kind of expectation of correspondence between theological assumption and literary form, see Robert Alter's treatment of the prose portions of the Hebrew Bible in his *The Art of Biblical Narrative* (New York, NY: Basic Books, 1981), pp. 19, 27, 29, 33.
2 Adolf von Harnack, *What is Christianity?* (New York, NY: Harper Torchbooks, 1957) pp. 149, 17.
3 See Ferdinand Christian Baur, *Epochs of Church Historiography*, Part One, in Peter Hodgson (ed.), *Ferdinand Christian Baur On the Writing of Church History* (New York, NY: Oxford University Press, 1968), for the way this sort of dualism between historical and non-historical is employed in Christian self-understanding before the modern period.
4 For this imperial understanding of the classic, see Frank Kermode, *The Classic* (Cambridge, MA: Harvard University Press, 1975), pp. 1–43.
5 See Ibid., pp. 38–45, 74–80, for this variant of an account of classic texts.
6 David Tracy, *The Analogical Imagination: Christian Theology and the Culture of Pluralism* (New York, NY: The Crossroad Publishing Company, 1987), pp. 125, 183 n. 22.
7 Ibid., p. 133
8 David Tracy, *Plurality and Ambiguity: Hermeneutics, Religion, Hope* (San Francisco, CA: Harper and Row, 1987), p. 86.
9 Tracy, *Analogical Imagination*, p. 108.
10 It is common in this connection to discuss the early theological interests of Heidegger and Gadamer.
11 Tracy, *Analogical Imagination*, pp. 171–172, 194.
12 Kermode, p. 114.
13 See Wolfgang Iser, "Indeterminacy and the Reader's Response," in J. Hillis Miller (ed.), *Aspects of Narrative: Selected Papers from the English Institute* (New York, NY: Columbia University Press, 1971), p. 43.
14 See Umberto Eco, *The Role of the Reader: Explorations in the Semiotics of Texts* (Bloomington, IN: Indiana University Press, 1979), pp. 49–50.
15 Ibid., pp. 47–48.
16 Christopher Norris, *Deconstruction* (London and New York: Methuen, 1982), p. 122; see also pp. 13–14, 20–21.

17 Ibid., pp. 13–14, 24.
18 For this identification of modernist reading, see Anthony Easthope, *Literary into Cultural Studies* (London and New York: Routledge, 1991), pp. 11–18.
19 *Mimesis: The Representation of Reality in Western Literature*, trans. Willard R. Trask (Princeton, NJ: Princeton University Press, 1953).
20 See Tracy, *Analogical Imagination*, pp. 108, 118, 122.
21 Ibid. pp. 175–177, 197, 200–201.
22 For Frei's distancing of himself from New Criticism, see George Hunsinger and William Placher (eds.), *Theology and Narrative: Selected Essays* (Oxford: Oxford University Press, 1993), pp. 140–143, esp. 141.
23 Frei seems, then, to replace the account of literary value in New Criticism with an account that refers to the normative standing of texts for particular communities. Unlike New Criticism or Tracy's hermeneutics, Frei's general account of the classic as a community formation does not generalize about the nature of classic texts and their readers, but simply points one to the particular features of texts and readers in the community at issue. In the Christian case (according to Frei), the classic texts happen to be narrative in form and readers happen to insist on the primacy of their literal sense. No general account of classic texts or their readers makes this a prerequisite for all classic texts.

    For my purposes here, however, the novelty of Frei's later position is less important than the way it allows him to retain so many of the features of New Criticism that he finds theologically appealing. The account of the classic in terms of normativity for a community is just a new means to much the same ends. The text still constructs its own world. In addition (though I do not discuss the points here), 1) the narrative features of the text retain their importance; 2) the text means what it says—there is no point to going behind it by some effort of historical reconstruction; and 3) the prerequisites for understanding classic texts remain minimal—anyone has interpretive access to a community's norms for reading by something analogous to an anthropological mode of description. See Frei, pp. 143–148.
24 See *Narratives of a Vulnerable God* (Louisville, KY: Westminster/John Knox Press, 1994), pp. 87–108.
25 See Alter. Reference to him in this context might seem odd in that one burden of his book is to show that biblical texts can be read as artful literary wholes. But I read him, I think not unfairly, with an emphasis on what sets off biblical narrative from our usual expectations about literary unity. See pp. 132–133. In this, what he says about the Hebrew Bible is quite similar to what Kermode says about *Wuthering Heights* in *The Classic*.
26 Kermode, p. 128
27 Ibid.
28 See Richard Hays, *Echoes of Scripture in the Letters of Paul* (New Haven, CT: Yale University Press, 1989).
29 Tracy perhaps comes closest to breaking this association. Because it is a human universal, every person—no matter how uneducated or unrefined—must live her life with reference to classic texts. Anything can thereby become a classic—not just masterpieces of world literature. The features that account for a classic are nevertheless defined by Tracy with such masterpieces in mind.
30 See Auerbach, "Sermo Humilis," in his *Literary Language and its Public in Late Antiquity and in the Middle Ages*, trans. Ralph Manheim (New York, NY: Pantheon, 1965). This point of Auerbach's is easy to miss because, although he discusses popular genres of writing (sermons, medieval liturgical plays), he is particularly interested in the influence of the Bible on texts that (unlike popular ones) strive for an elevated or high style in their depiction of everyday events. Auerbach in this sense, too, then, encourages the drawing of parallels between the Bible and Western works of high-culture artistry.

    Whether the Bible violates standards of high-culture artistry is in part, of course, an historical question since such standards vary. E.g., although they continue to have a major influence on Western literature, some aspects of the Greco-Roman standards—notably, the correlation of style with subject matter are later lost. Despite this historical variation, the general points made by Auerbach about popular texts (which I follow in the rest of this paragraph of my text) would seem, however, to remain germane, especially for the Bible. For example, the Bible is not generally written in a high style, that is, in a pretentious and erudite style that serves to limit its audience; there is an immediacy and directness about its account of the everyday which is different from the "view from above" treatment typical of high culture texts when they recount ordinary events of life; and matters of extraordinary significance are treated as if they were continuous with those of everyday experience (i.e., events of ordinary life seem the entrance way even to matters of hidden and mysterious consequence). See Auerbach, *Mimesis*, pp. 89–93, 151–168.

31   *Epistles* 137.18, trans. by Auerbach, "Sermo," p. 50.
32   John Fiske, *Understanding Popular Culture* (London and New York: Routledge, 1989), pp. 122, 147–148.
33   Ibid., p. 109.
34   Ibid., p. 124.
35   This is a central argument of Easthope's book.
36   See Fiske, pp. 103–127.
37   See Pierre Bourdieu, *Distinction: A Social Critique of the Judgement of Taste*, trans. Richard Nice (Cambridge, MA: Harvard University Press, 1984).
38   Kermode, p. 134, slightly altered; see also pp. 132–133.
39   Compare Roland Barthes, *Criticism and Truth* (Minneapolis, MN: University of Minnesota Press, 1987), pp. 72–74.
40   The important contribution that historical-critical investigation of the Bible could make to widening the churches' biblical imagination in this way should be obvious. How the Bible might be interpreted as a guide to life in the present is broadened by a knowledge of how the Bible was so used in the past, by a knowledge of what it meant to its original audiences, by a knowledge of the diversity of voices to be heard in its various books, etc.
41   Some of these worrisome readings are popular readings, in the sense that they are widespread and/or produced by people who are not elite in educational background and/or institutional religious standing. One can therefore use an understanding of biblical authority that is informed by contemporary theories of popular texts to contest some popular readings—those that validate their own readings by undercutting what it is about this text that makes it popular and therefore open to more than a single sort of reading.

Index

Printed and bound by CPI Group (UK) Ltd, Croydon, CR0 4YY

09/06/2025

14686132-0005